A FAMILIAR DIALOGUE OF THE FRIEND AND THE FELLOW

EARLY ENGLISH TEXT SOCIETY

No. 295

1989

A FAMILIAR DIALOGUE OF THE FRIEND AND THE FELLOW

A Translation of Alain Chartier's
Dialogus Familiaris Amici et Sodalis

EDITED BY

MARGARET S. BLAYNEY

Published for
THE EARLY ENGLISH TEXT SOCIETY
by the
OXFORD UNIVERSITY PRESS
LONDON   NEW YORK   TORONTO
1989

Oxford University Press, Walton Street, Oxford OX2 6DP

Oxford New York Toronto
Delhi Bombay Calcutta Madras Karachi
Petaling Jaya Singapore Hong Kong Tokyo
Nairobi Dar es Salaam Cape Town
Melbourne Auckland

and associated companies in
Beirut Berlin Ibadan Nicosia

Oxford is a trade mark of Oxford University Press

British Library Cataloguing in Publication Data

Chartier, Alain, ca 1385–ca 1433
[Dialogus familiarus amici et sodalis.
Middle English]. A familiar dialogue of the
friend and the fellow: a translation of
Alain Chartier's Dialogus familiarus amici
et sodalis.—(Early English Text Society; no. 295)
I. Title   II. Blayney, Margaret S. (Margaret Statler), 1926–
878'.0408
ISBN 0-19-722297-8

Printed in Great Britain by,
Richard Clay Ltd, Bungay, Suffolk

CONTENTS

INTRODUCTION

AMONG the works of Alain Chartier (*c.*1385-1433) related to the social and political problems of the struggles between France and England during his lifetime was *Dialogus familiaris amici et sodalis super deploratione gallicae calamitatis*,[1] written about 1425. This Latin dialogue, along with Chartier's French prose works *Le Quadrilogue Invectif* and *Le Traité de l'Esperance, ou Consolation des Trois Vertus*,[2] was translated into English during the second half of the fifteenth century, all three probably by the same author, possibly Sir John Fortescue, although this attribution is far from certain.

In *A Famylyer Dyaloge of the Freende and the Felaw vppon the Lamentacion of the Myserable Calamyte of Fraunce*, the Freende asks the Felaw why he is so overcome with sorrow. The Felaw explains that he laments the ruinous condition of France, caused by the corruption and vices, especially covetice and ambition, of the rulers, the army, and the common people. The Freende tries to convince the Felaw that he should be more ordinate in his grief and be happy in his own prosperity and position of high esteem. But to emphasize his despair about the conditions in France, the Felaw uses the effective image of a ship about to be wrecked because of broken oars, torn sails, and an ill-formed rudder. He says that every man should put the welfare of the country before his own private welfare and risk everything for the honour of his country. The two companions then discuss not only the situation in France, but the judgements of God in regard to their own country and its enemies, and end with a consideration of the meaning and possibilities of peace, with the Felaw again taking a less hopeful attitude than the Freende. The Felaw argues that more than external peace is

---

[1] Edited by Georg Rosenthal (Halle, 1901). The translation has been compared with this edition.

[2] See *English Translations of Alain Chartier's Le Traité de l'Esperance and Le Quadrilogue Invectif*, ed. Margaret S. Blayney, EETS, i. 270 (1974), ii. 281 (1980), for further discussions of Chartier works, the English manuscripts, the authorship of the translations, and the manner of translation.

needed; inner peace, which exists only in an ordered state and the concord of all citizens, is all important. All in all, the *Dyaloge*, like *The Quadrilogue Invective* and *The Treatise of Hope*, reveals, through the views of the Felaw, Chartier's unhappiness and even despair about the evils in France during this period.

The *Dyaloge* is found in the following English manuscripts:

London: Sion College MS. L. 40.2/E 43, ff. 39–58ᵛ (S), the copy text for this edition;

Cambridge: St. John's College MS. 76. D 1, ff. 27ᵛ–41ᵛ (J);

Chicago: Newberry Library MS. f. 36, Ry 20, ff. 23ᵛ–32ᵛ (N).

It does not appear in Rawlinson (Bodleian Library) MS. A. 338, where *The Quadrilogue* and *The Treatise of Hope* are found. S and J, as discussed in the introduction to the editions of *The Quadrilogue* and *The Treatise of Hope*, are closely related manuscripts, probably copied from the same exemplar, while N appears to be of a different family.

If the translations of *The Quadrilogue*, *The Treatise of Hope*, and the *Dyaloge* are by the same author as seems likely, he appears to have had a somewhat better command of Latin than he had of French, although the *Dyaloge* shows the same freedom of translation, the same interesting vocabulary, and the same often forceful prose style noted in the other two translations.

TREATMENT OF THE TEXT

THE treatment of the text is in general the same as in the editions of the English translations of *Le Traité de l'Esperance* and *Le Quadrilogue Invectif*. The additions accepted in S from the other manuscripts when NJ agree are placed in square brackets and are not recorded in the critical apparatus. The corrections in S are placed in parentheses and are also not recorded unless NJ have different readings. I have recorded only substantive variants, with certain exceptions noted below. Thus, I have recorded all additions and omissions when NJ differ from S; transpositions, since N especially shows a tendency for such rearrangement of words; and differences in singular and plural forms. I have not recorded words and forms commonly interchanged by these and other scribes (e.g. 'ofttymes'—'oftentymes', 'parte'—'party', whosoeuyr'—'whosomeuyr'). I have also not recorded minor obviously scribal errors in NJ (e.g. dittography errors, omissions of a single letter, insertions, or cancellations in NJ), unless they seem to reveal something about the relationship of the manuscripts. I have punctuated and capitalized according to modern usage, and I have expanded meaningful abbreviations and contractions without comment. I have emended a reading that occurs in all the manuscripts only occasionally, then to follow the Latin or to attempt to make sense of what appears to be an obvious corruption.

A Famylyer Dyaloge of the Freende and the Felaw vppon the Lamentacion of the Myserable Calamyte of Fraunce

What ys yt, my moste trusty frende, that bysyde thyn
accustomed maner stondyng aferre othyrwyse than ys syt- 5
tynge to the, causyng the to stonde as a man wythowt voyce,
whyche semes that thou art not lyke the same man that thou
hast ben aforetyme? Thou art yn the case of a goode cyteseyn
hauynge of the peple goode name and goode fame. Thou
stondyst amonge the states and noblys yn grete favour 10
wythowt any hurte. Thyr ys in the grete yndustry of study
and of lyterature plente thorough whyche thou mayst rewle
thy soule and comfort thyself yn al maner of daungeres. Thou
hast freendes also whose counseyl and goodes thou mayst vse
after the maner as trewe frendeschyp requereth. Thou art not 15
charged wyth the comon wele, and yf y vnderstonde aryght
thy sobre attemperaunce and thy goodes suffyce the suche
wyse that they excede not to provoke envye, and they suffyce
yn suche wyse also that thou lakkest nothyng that ys to the
necessary. Yn eloquence and prudence þou hast many folowers, 20
fewe better or egal. Thou art free born. þou condytest thy lyfe
noblye, wroth wyth no man but wyth suche as ben contraryous
to vertu whome to dysplese ys but very preysyng. Thou art
hoole yn age, hoole yn body, yf þou wylt not wylfully wex
furyouse abatyng thy vygour. But what ys yt that th[u]s 25
troubleth the and causeth the to wex leene, as ho seyth, thou
castest hedely downe thy floryschyng youthe, and causeth the
to seeme as a man ronne yn age? O thou fatal sustyr Attropos,
þou hatest thyn offyce. Attropos schulde not come hastely lest
sche breke the threde or yt be perfytely wownde vp. Do 30
therfor, my frende, as ys accordyng to a vygorous man / and f. 40
as goodely as thou mayst, passe thys lyfe, whych ys breef and
trancytory. The tragedye cryeth, 'Why lyst the goddes not to

3 Freende] Auctour SJ *om*. N Aimicus L   4 trusty] trysty J   25 thus]
NJ thys S   26 the (1)] *om*. N   27 castest] casteth NJ   28 ronne] fer
add. N   fatal] fittal J   29 þou . . . Attropos] *om*. N

suffre the peple to lyue ioyfully, for lyfe hasteth hymself by hys course assigned?' For thyr is no man vnder the sonne that hath more of hys labour but lyue wel and be glad and ioyful.

THE FELAWE

Thou spekest in lyke wyse as though yt were oon maner of 5 thynge seyeng and doyng.

THE FREENDE

I iuge not so, but ryghtwysnes and equite of thynges causeth eese to men accustomed to vertu, and yn contrary wyse vnequyte doth dysplesyr and vyolence.   10

THE FELAWE

We ar men and thyr is amonge oureself an ynwarde batayle, but who ys he that hath borne awey the vyctory ayenst hys ynwarde enemy?

THE FREENDE   15

Thou art not as the flokke and freel multytude of men nor the executour and folower of thy passyouns, but forasmoche as thou surmovntest othyr men yn vertu so rewle the be thyn owne soule.

THE FELAWE   20

Wolde God y wer suche wyth myself as y am anest the. Neuertheles whatesomeuer we bothe be I knowe wel we be but men and no goddes.

THE FRENDE

And though we may not atteyne to the goddes ynmortall as 25 yn dygnyte, yet vertu maketh vs parteneres and folowers of the godhede.

THE FELAW

Thou beleuest wel, for the folkes that ben set yn nobley thorough the celestyal vygour clothen hemself wyth dyvyne 30 strenght, as yt apperyth by the seyenge of Omer, the poete,

---

21 am] ne *add*. N   anest] anenst NJ   25 ynmortall] ymmortall J
30 hemself] hyrself J

where he called and named Hector the chylde of god for hys / f. 40ᵛ
grete vertu. Also the noble dyvyne and hystoriagrafe Varo
seyde, 'Yt is no voyde feyth to sey thyr be a kynde of goddes.'
But where be suche godly men nowadayes?

THE FREENDE   5

Though we may not be goddes yet as moche as we may we
ought to folow (hem).

THE FELAW

Thou seyst ryght wele, but yt ys a merveyle yf thou
perfourme the same.   10

THE FREENDE

To iuge myself ys but an errour, but yet y dar ryght wele
ascrybe to myself that whatsomeuer y am I wulde fayne lyue
ioyfully.

THE FELAW   15

Thou art happy and prosperous yf thou excede not mesure
whan thou art yn gladnes, for the lyfe of glad peple ys as a
slyper way for when he wulde reteyne hymself he schal not
inow do yt.

THE FREENDE   20

Peryl ys ouyral. Neuertheles yn that case yt ys more
vncomodyouse to enclyne to heuynes than to gladnes.

THE FELAW

Eutropolya hath vnto bothe partyes hys maneres, places
and tymes. Thyr ys bothe tyme of laughyng and tyme of 25
wepyng, and ho that dothe the contrary vseth the offyce of a
iaper or a iangler and not of a wyse man, and also the meene of
vertu ys not egal to al thynges nor to al men, for that þat lakkes
at oon tyme ouyrfloweth anothyr tyme.

---

2 hystoriagrafe] hystoriaagrafe J historagrafe N   3 be] is (*perhaps canc.*)
be N   4 godly] *om.* N   7 hem] hym *canc.* hem *ins.* S   13 fayne]
om. N   17 as] *om.* N   28 þat] at J

THE FREENDE

Thou hast seyde holsomly, but yet kepe not secrete from
me why thou hast chaunged the maner of thy lyfe.

THE FELAW

As tymes be, so be maneres. 5

THE FREENDE

Thou schewest inconstaunce.

THE FELAW

I beleve yt ys a vertu to mesure yn maner the soule wyth
tyme. 10

THE FREENDE

I ley the famous man Socrates ayenst the, whyche was
called ryght vertuous, of whome bothe yn aduercyte and yn
prosperite was of oon manere of countenaunce ynsomoche
that whan he had ressayued hys drynke of dethe yet betwene 15
the dyspeyre of lyfe and deth he dysputyd and taught his / f. 41
dyssyples wyth glad chere and wythoute abaschynge of any
countenaunce.

THE FELAW

Thou schowest me of a man whyche at al tymes had a grete 20
ʒele to the comon wele, and on a tyme he was so meued wyth
errour of the same that he provoked the wreth of hys
cyteseynes and prepared deth to hymself.

THE FREENDE

Now y vnderstonde wherefor thou art meved, for I se wel 25
thou ordeynest for thyself and wythyn thyself a secret
heuynes for þe domage of the comon wele.

THE FELAW

Who, I pray the, ys of so yren an herte or norysched vp
wyth the mylke of wylde beestes but at he may sorow the falle 30
and the ruyne of the wele publyke?

14 was] *om.* N   oon] ? god N   25 Now] Mow N   30 at] þat N

THE FREENDE

I knowe certeyn that yt ys for the and al other goode men to loue the comon wele.

THE FELAW

Wherefor than dost þou blame me? 5

THE FREENDE

For thou dost othyrwyse than ys accordynge to thyn age and also þou kepest no mesure.

THE FELAW

Thou menest wel in thynges pryvat, but who may make 10 euyn wyth teeres þe chaunce and the ruyne of the comon wele?

THE FREENDE

In al extremytes yt ys the maner of a wyse man to declyne and tempre hymself. 15

THE FELAW

Abyde awhyle I beseche the. Art thou remembred that þou hast euer rad the volumes of the olde fadres?

THE FREENDE

Wolde God that I had as wel vnderstonde hem as I haue 20 redde hem.

THE FELAW

And yf thou vnderstodest hem parfytely, thou woldest knowe thyself convyct yf þou haddest redde wyth how bytter soules oure olde fadres haue borne the iniuries as wel of 25 goddes ynmortal as of the comon wele.

THE FREENDE

I haue it wele yn remembrance.

2 goode] *om*. N   7 to] for N

THE FELAW

Than thou must of necessite knowlyche these iniuryes not only to haue / ben compleyned wythoute mesure but also to haue made oure fadrys the more feerce. f. 41ᵛ

THE FREENDE　　　　　　　　5

I vnderstonde wel theffecte of that seyenge, but I wulde that thou schuldest reduce þe same thyng more pleynly vnto my mynde.

THE FELAW

Thyr ar al redy and at honde copy of ensamples. 10

THE FREENDE

Schewe me oon al only.

THE FELAW

Thou hast herde how þat noble and famous man Scypyo Affrycan did whan Hanybal swelled yn tryvmphes and 15 beseged Roome.

THE FREENDE

I am ygnoraunte. Thou hast begonne.

THE FELAW

Whenne the noble fadres of Roome wer beseged and 20 destytute of hope, consentyd to haue forsake the cyte, the seyde Scypyo with a couragyous herte pulled oute hys sworde yn myddes of the counseyle protestyng wyth othe publyke that whosomeuyr aftyr that spake any more of leuyng of the cyte or forsakyng schulde lose hys hede. Also he reteyned the 25 folkes fugytyfe yn a grete furye.

THE FREENDE

I haue redde the same and ryght so ys the lettre yn the boke called Tytus Lyvyus.

14 þat] the *add.* J　　Scypyo] Stypyo J *unclear* N

THE FELAW

How than brake owt thys most noble man wyth a feruent angre yn oppen counseyle where the soule ought to be fre wythoute bondage of any passyoun, where manere pees and grevousnes ought to be kept and obserued, but oonly 5 forasmoche as that the offences publyke excede the manere and mesure of mans hardynesse and yre, for they can neuer be sorowfully ynough bewepte nor egyrly ynough avenged.

THE FREENDE

Thou seyst ryght. 10

THE FELAW

Moreouer þou hast a sygne and ensample yn þe Olde Testament whereas they schewed by teryng of / ther clothes, f. 42 blasphemed her god, named doo[m]e, yn offence of þe name of God or the lawe, as though they schewed not only to bere 15 the iniuryes heuely but rathyr wexed as wylde and woode for the wronges done to the comon wele and al greves and sadnesses forsake and set apparte for helpyng of the seyde comon wele.

THE FREENDE 20

Now I vndirstonde wele thy conclusion of suche thynges as þou hast askyd me, but I knewe neuer such iniuries that wer so grete whyche schulde cause to yssew owt of thy mouthe so grete complayntes and inordenat weymentynges.

THE FELAW 25

Allas, allas, thou schewest as though þou knewe not suche thynges but lyke as taught and vntaught dwellers and straungers speke opynly togedre.

THE FREENDE

What though I knowe not, yet wulde y vnderstonde what 30 thou knowest yn thys case.

---

4 where] ani *add.* N   6 excede] exceded J
unclear N   14 doome] doone SJ *unclear* N
18 sadnesses . . . set] sadnesse layde N
30 wulde y] I will N   8 ynough (1)] be *add.* SJ
     16 for] for *add.* S
24 weymentynges] *sing.* N

THE FELAW

Who of peryschyng schypmen knoweth not the comon peryl?

THE FREENDE

To me y wote ys an vnwysedom not for to knowe, but to 5
the, knowyng and questyoned, not to onswer ys but dys-
deyne.

THE FELAW

And yf thou wylt that I wyth wordes schall renovel ageyne
myne inestymable sorow, I schall take the way that thou 10
commaundest.

THE FREENDE

Procede y pray the.

THE FELAW

Thyr was neuer lyfe more hevy to men nor dethe lasse to be 15
dradde than to me and to the peple of thys reme, whose
spyrytes of lyfe ben kept wyth grete yrksomnes, and yt
schulde seeme that a wykkyd sterre and constellacion appered
whenne we were borne to thys comon wele. But and faate had
pourveyde oure dethe that we schulde not haue seene these 20
grete euylles or els Lucyna, the goddesse, had reserued oure
natal dayes vnto / lenger processe of yerys, yt had be wele. f. 42ᵛ
But yet y wote not what bettyr sesons we may trust, for the
noughty men promytte vs acursed and an vnhappy posterite.
Yf yt so be that nature by an ynfenyte myght brynge forthe 25
lyke thynges of lyke, whate maner of sones schal com forthe
aftyr or what successours schal folow of suche parentes? Oure
eldres had the golden worlde and theyr posteryte chaunged yt
ynto syluer and after þat ynto brasse, and now fynally we
chaunge yt ynto vyces, oure age polute wyth stynkyng fylthes, 30
wyth ynfamye and to be abhorred wyth al pure soules,
whyche horrours and stynkes may wel be called the stenche of
the weyght of nature. The Frensche name afore thys tyme

---

2 peryschyng] of *add*. N   6 questyoned] queste nyd J   20 haue] a N
22 natal] naturall N   23 not] *om*. N

was to vs glorious and to straungeres honorable, and we be
now heuy and chargeable to oureself and laughen to scorne
wyth al othyr peple. Oure eldres succeded and enheryted
aftyr theyre auncestres. In vertu, glory and honour they kepte
that was left hem aftyr theyr progenytours encresed that came 5
to theyre possession. And we prowde wastours of oure
prosperyte corrupte and dystroye al þat we fynde of oure
formefadyrs, fyndynge newe meenes to hurte oure owne
wele. We haue ben hote and brennynge yn the begynnynge of
batayles; we haue erred yn condyteng of the same; we haue 10
erred yn þe endynge of hem. Wyth how gret study haue we
norysched cyuyle batayles we haue yn experyence, and yet to
thys ynwarde fyre we haue mynestred secretly þe sulphyr of
falce subtylte and desseyte. O freel soules, to the destruccion
of Frenschemen and obstynat resystyng ayenst vertu! Som- 15
tyme batayles chastysed and amended not only oure eldres
but also othyr straunge peple dulle yn vertu, but oure batayles
haue corrupte and made vs worse. Batayles of olde tyme
repressyd lechery and synful lustes, but yn oure tyme they
expresse and make open lustes of synne. Batayle somtyme 20
excyted and quyk/kened the vertu of men, but yn oure tyme f. 43
they excyte men to plesant softnes and slowthe. Othyr
mennes vygour and vertu ys made parfyte yn ynfyrmyte and
aduercyte; oure vertu yn aduercyte ys confounded and
quenched. In tyme passed whan oure comon wele dyd 25
florysche, wurschipful rewardes and lawdes were yeuen and
ordeyned to suche as had deserued hem vertuously, but
nowadayes rychesse chalangeth the pryce, and pouerte,
though yt be vertuouse, ys repreuable and set at nought. We
calle yt now wysedom and encrese suche as ys synguler wele, 30
and thyr ys now a newe invencion of men and a chaunge
from the olde polecye, and that is to plukke away by craft
the comon rychesse, whych men teche her sones, rathyr
than lettreture. Feerful and hedy aventuryng, medled with
presumpcion and ynyquite, ys now called the vertu of 35
strengthe. And outewarde oure enemyes make vs werre
thorough whyche we be dyssesed of oure possessyons, and
the pestelence of vyces maketh oure ynwarde batayles.

3 wyth] of N   5 hem] ? hym N   10 batayles] *sing.* N   11 how]
oute N   haue we] *tr.* N   32 by craft] *om.* N   34 hedy] hevy J

Befortyme manly men of armes desereden to seche glory by
doyng of armes and so by theyre excellence was made of hem
memorye thorough honorable fame, levyng to her folowers
and successours sygnes, ymages, tables and grete rychesses
goten of her enemyes to encrese her courage (to) do lyke actes. 5
But werryours of oure tyme leve to her chyldren a most vyle
and schamefull memoryal whyche of ryght ought to be called
the spectacle of vyces, that ys to say, vengable brennyng,
horryble mvrdre[s], abhomynable dyffowlyng of women,
raveynouse extorcions, and sacrylege. Turne thyn yghen 10
aboute the yn compase and lyft vp thyn eeres, and thou schalt
heere and see on euery syde thynges merueylyously foule to
the syght and horrebely to be herde, for opynly and pryvatly
we al be abused; we / haue yndyfferently the ryght for the   f. 43ᵛ
wronge and þe wronge for the ryght. Coveytyce and ambycion 15
haue the preemynence and souereynte yn the comon wele that
he may þerby encrese hys pryvate weele. We confounde and
medyl togedre devyne thynges and humayne thynges ayenst
al ordre. We offre to þe halowes to thentente that we may
accheue oure cursed and vnhappy appetytes. Who yn thys 20
dayes wexeth reede for schame of syn? Who ys abasched for
drede of iugement? Whatsomeuyr lyketh vs we beleve yt ys to
vs leful. But what fruyte or effecte of labour may we accheue
or atteyne to by thys maner of craftes? What ende and
conclusyon ys dewe to suche maners? I see fyrebrondes and 25
wastful fyres redy to oure hondes thorough whych oure
comoun wele schall brenne. I see myserable sepultures and
tereful ruyne remayne as parpetual sygnes to Frenschemen
for theyre grete schame. Oure noble men falle yn batayle.
Oure contre ys yn dekay. Batayles dayly encrese of custome. 30
The strengthe of oure vertu peryscheth. We falle vtterly. And
so y covnte that whosomeuer passeth these dayes gladly
doth as he that syngenge and ioyenge foloweth hys fadyrs
lamentable corps to hys beryenge. Suffre me therfor to
beweepe the falle of the comon wele, and syn the self thyng 35

1 Befortyme] aforetyme N   desereden] desyred N   2 doyng] of dedys add. N
5 courage] corages N   6 chyldren] chyldre J   9 mvrdres] NJ mvrdrers
S   dyffowlyng] diffoyling N   13 pryvatly] pryvely N   14 for] from N
15 for] fro N   20 thys] þais N   22 Whatsomeuyr] it add. N
23 fruyte] fuyrte N   26 whych] om. J   29 grete] om. N   30 contre]
courte N   dekay] dekays N

scheweth mater of wepynge (meve) me not sodeynly to gladnes.

THE FREENDE

Art thou so harde set yn thy purpos that thou wylt here no mannes reson othyrwyse than thyn appetyte iugeth?   5

THE FELAW

No, for rathyr y wyl not here for bothe yt yrketh me and schameth me that the name of gladnes schulde entremedyl / f. 44 hymself with heuy thynges.

THE FREENDE   10

The soules of wyse men schew hemself yn þat that they bere harde and heuy thynges temporatly.

THE FELAW

Yn thys mater to kepe mesure me thenketh no temperaunce.

THE FREENDE   15

What profyte ys yt to the and to the comon wele that thyself perysche therwyth?

THE FELAW

Wolde God that I myght perysche for yt and not wyth yt, lyke as the sentence was of Camilus, the grete counseyler of 20 Roome. 'Y pray,' seyde he, 'and beseche the Godly mynde, yf the celestyal bodyes enforce anythyng to do a gretter euyl ayenst the comon wele that they excecute and fulfille theyre operacion ayenst my brede and my housholde so that therby the comon wele myght be esed of theyr peyne.' We ar not 25 better than the famous Caton, yn whose age thyr leued none more excellent yn vertu, whyche myght not suffre noon offence ayenst the comon wele and liberte of the same but fledde away to a cyte name Vtyke yn Lybye and there wylfully with a draught of poyson hasted hys last day. Nor oure lyfe 30 also ys not more wurthy than the lyff of that noble Romeyn

---

1 meve] *written above* meene S   26 thyr] *om.* N   none] no N

knyght named Marcus Curcyus, whych wylfully payed for
the redempcion and the helthe of the comon wele of Roome.

THE FREENDE

Thou hast spoken pytuously. Neuertheles y counseyle the
that thou be rathyr aboute to delyuer and saue the from the 5
comon peryl and thyn owne peryl also, and aftyr that whan
thou hast opportunite and space, than counseyle and helpe
the comon wele.

THE FELAW

Thou mevest as though [the] hope of the comon wele were 10
al yn me.

THE FREENDE

Y meve the rathyr to be of goode herte as a man, partener of
eyther fortvne, that ys to say prosperyte and aduercyte, and yf 14
thou / seest a dowte of the comon wele, þou, as nygh as thou f. 44
mayst, be delygent to fynde a seurte for thyn owne lyvyng and
yeve thy counseyle to the comon wele.

THE FELAW

Yn that case y may sorow for yt.

THE FREENDE   20

Not only yn that but þou mayst exorte othyr by thy wurde
as þou canst right wele and art manly yn soule to do yt.

THE FELAW

What ys more sluggysche and dulle than deefe men? Fewe
thyr be that nowadayes applye to turne theyre studyes to the 25
comon wele. Vnnethe thyr be any that wyl suffre to be taught
yn that behalfe.

THE FREENDE

Thou spekest merueylous[l]y, and myne oppynyon ys
accordyng to the same, for he lyveth not fruytefully that 30
levyth al for hymself.

---

1 payed] dyed N   11 al] *om.* N   15 þou] *om.* N   29 merueylously]
J merueylousy S merveouslye N

THE FELAW

Thou seyst trewe and ouyr that y say that he ys an vnholsom cyteseyne whych ys neglygent to the comon wele, but now yt ys turned to a comon vyce for moche peple deffendeth yt to be called for a vertu, suche wyse that the 5 vnyuersal wele may not encrese wyth vs.

THE FREENDE

Y holde that ryght an euyl errour, for wheresomeuyr þou seest plente of rychesse yn synguler persones there the name and the comon wele ys set apart.   10

THE FELAW

Now felest thou what maketh me hevy, for we see before the sygnes euydently appere of falce coniecture. Wolde God that these sygnes schewe not trewly before what schall folow.   15

THE FREENDE

A schyp oftentymes ys lyke to go to wrakke whyche afterward fortunably happeth to arryve at a goode porte. The chaunces folow not alway lyke to the manaces that schewe before.   20

THE FELAW

Thou schewest ensamples ryght conuenyently.

THE FREENDE

Me semes that y do so.

THE FELAW   25

And now y wyl returne thys ensample agaynst the yf so be that þou wylt answer to my questyon.

THE FREENDE

Haue do and procede.

12 what] that N   maketh] make N

THE FELAW

Who may / trust the welefare of a schyp whyche ys toward　f. 45
a wrakke and the ores be broken or the mast kyt or the sayle
ouyral rent or the gouernayle vnproporcyoned?

THE FREENDE　　　　　　　　　　　　　　　　5

Forsothe no man.

THE FELAW

Ryght so oure comon wele ressembleth a shyppe whyche ys
destytute of al suche thynges as ys aforeseyde, for we haue no
suche wysedom nor prudence wythyn vs whych putteth 10
maner and ordre to the gouernayle to condyte þe schyp by a
dewe meene, and also we despyse vttyrly to lerne or here the
wysedom of hem that haue yt.

THE FREENDE

That ys vnsyttynge, for as Tyrence seythe, thou schuldest 15
asaye alle thyng by counseyle fyrst or þou assaye hem by
armes, for wysedom, whatsomeuyr aventure of fortune falle,
maketh men sure, and a prudent and a (fre) soule yn
counseylyng ys most sure fyrmament for a comon wele.

THE FELAW　　　　　　　　　　　　　　　　20

Seke anothyr seurte and fyrmament, for that ys vanyssched
ynto the practyke of Ȝerces, the kyng of Perce, whyche
schewed vnto hys peple and seyde, 'Syres,' quod he, 'y haue
called yow togedre lest that yt be thought y do thys acte allone
wythoute counseyle. Neuyrtheles remembre yow that youre 25
part ys rathyr to obeye than to parsuade.'

THE FREENDE

Thou schewest the begynnyng of gret calamyte, but y prey
the pursewe the remnaunt of the ensamples that þou spakest
of before.　　　　　　　　　　　　　　　　　　　　30

---

2 whyche] om. N　　　　　3 be] om. N　　　　18 fre] written above clere S
29 that] om. N

THE FELAW

Y schal do yt yn fewe wordes. We bere broken ores yf we
dyssolue temperaunce wyth superfluouse eese and delycacyes,
whyche vertu of attempraunce makyth euyn the qualytees of
the soule and tempreth hem wyth dewe proporcion and 5
couenable mevyng. We lyft vp the sayle rent on euery syde yf
we enlarge iustice / for (favour) or rygorously restreyne yt f. 45ᵛ
for malyce or envye, for lyke as the sayle ys lassened or
enlarged after the quantyte of þe wynde and peyseth the
schyppe by mesure, so iustyce egally mesured to euery man 10
conserueth the equyte of the poletyke body and the wele
publyke. We lyft vp a broken mast yf oure nobles gentyles be
ouerthrowe yn batayle or elles yf vnordenat lustes and
corrupte maners haue broken the vertu of the soules of oure
strong and wurthy men.   15

THE FREENDE

Whyles thys maner of dysposycions ys amonges vs, though
the helthe publyke desyre to be saued yt may not, and therefor
seece and serche no ferther.

THE FELAW   20

Now sorow casteth oute the teres, and the syghes and the
sobbynges constreyne and lette the wey of speche. Sorow hyd
yn þe herte ys enemy to speche. Drede of thynges to come
greve sore oure present thoughtes, for beleue ys euer redy and
adioyned to drede yn peynefull thynges.   25

THE FREENDE

Yet cast not away hope for oftentymes yt hath ben holsom
to trust wele.

THE FELAW

Yt ys a freel solas where alle thynges fayle saue only hope. 30

THE FREENDE

Forsothe and hope may be trewe.

7 favour] *written above* favor S   8 ys] ? be N   or] be *add*. N   12 yf]
if *add*. N   13 vnordenat] inordynate N   18 therefor] ther J
22 sobbynges] ? sobyng N   24 greve] greveth N   25 yn] is N

THE FELAW

Yt ys trouthe.

THE FREENDE

The power of the goddes ys egal as yt hath bene before, and
the hevenly wrathe may be aswaged and the chere of fortune 5
chaunged.

THE FELAW

Thou hast seyde lykely wordes yf þou canst inow chaunge
the maners of man. Thou hast herde what the famous man
Salust seyth, 'Yf thou yeue the to slowthe and cowardyse, 10
thou prayest yn veyne to the goddes for to avaunce thy cause,
for yn that case they ere wrothe and sore meved.'

THE FREENDE

I herde of my fadyr yn the presence of myn eldres þat were 14
wyse men and also so / of chyldehode y was taught that grete f. 46
dyscordes haue ofttymes wasted oure reeme but neuer lost yt.

THE FELAW

The batayles that thou spekest of wasted the bodyes of
men, but the batayles that be had nowadayes and the
dyscordes haue take awey the soules and vertuous maners. 20
And yn the batayles of tyme past men were constreyned to
vertu, but yn oure cyuyle and ynward batayles that now ben
vsed the vertues be ouercome and vyces reygne yn vyctoryous
tryvm[p]he. Reemes perysche not by dethe only of men, for
that that ys taken away by the vnpyte of man thorough theyre 25
cruelte yn batayle yet nature restoryth that ageyne by
generacion. Also the freele humanyte of the bodyes maketh
not stable the kyngdoms but the celestyal vertu, whyche ys a
yeft of God sprongen owt of the eternal sees, stablyscheth
erthely thynges, and how moche more men take of þe clerenes 30
therof, so moche more ar they parteners of þe durynge of
ther eternyte.

THE FREENDE

Thou serchest to profoundely.

9 man] þat J   15 so] ? om. N   28 kyngdoms] kyndoms N

THE FELAW

Profounde sorow maketh a grete wyt and euyr yn harde
thynges the gretter argvynge.

THE FRENDE

Yt ys leful to serche any more how that thys that thou 5
callest cyuyle batayles hurteth and taketh more of vs than
othyr batayles.

THE FELAW

Thou askest ful couenable questyons of the mater, whyche
may bothe provoke hevynes and opyn tereful compleyntes. 10

THE FREENDE

Procede ferther.

THE FELAW

Yt ys not so grete losse of goodes as of men ne of men as of
þe soules.   15

THE FREENDE

Sey forthe the remnant.

THE FELAW

Graunte a lytel leysyr to my wordes.

[THE FREENDE]   20

Than sey what thou / wylt, and y schalle bynde me to here f. 46ᵛ
what þou seyst.

THE FELAW

The Grekes somtyme whyles the worlde was subdued vnto
hem they had amonge hemself lyterature and studyes. They 25
had also the poletyke wysedom of lyuenge. They had þe
propre way of spekyng and eloquence and also the dyssyplyne
of batayles and cheualry, yn whych they surmountyd alle
othyr nacyons and peple. And alle these vertues, yndustry

---

14 of (2)] som *add*. N   20 The Freende] J and SN   23 Felaw]
Frende N   28 batayles] armes N

and prowesse the Romeyns wythdrewe from the Grekes, that
ys to sey the empyre and the gloryes of the worlde, and for
nothyng elles but only for ther vertu, for loke what wey that
vertu translateth hemself the empyres and poletyke wyse-
doms folowen. Yet aftyr that for lak of vertu and also for the 5
demerytes of oure noble auncestres the Lorde Almyghty
translated the lettres, þe study of the Grekes, the lawes of
mannes lyueng and the manere of knyghthode from they[m]
vnto vs, and therfor we haue had grete merveyle to thenke
that they be now as folkes destytute, dysolate and forsaken to 10
falle so hugely from the grete honour, connyng and vertu.
After hem florysched oure comon wele, and yn alle maner
thynges whedyr it tuched pees or batayle oure name was
exalted and magnyfyed. We had at þat tyme men of large
stature, stronge yn soule, hygh yn wysedom, sad and asseured 15
yn langage and merveylous grete doers yn execucion of
iustyce, whome the loue of vertu and dewe composycion of
ordres and maners made hem noble yn fame and renomee.
Allas, allas, by the chaunge of thynges and maners we that be
vnderstondyng knowe that the favour of fortune ys plukked 20
awey from vs, for we norysche nowadayes men lytel yn
stature, lasse yn soule, groce and erthely yn vnderstondyng,
femenyne yn wordes, freel and vnstable yn werkes. Lyterature
and connyng ys despyced, / and yet whosoeuyr savoureth yn f. 47
connyng let hym savour wele and fee[d]e hymself, and yn hys 25
talent and wysedome he schal be the hungryer yn these oure
last dayes. By fortune and hedynes wythoute concyderacion
yt ys assended to the gouernaunce of the comon wele, and
euery man hath theryn as grete largesse and lycence as he hath
hardynes and boldenes wythoute vndyrstondyng of hys 30
merytes, and the lawe of oure poletyke lyff at these dayes ys
euery man to take alle that he may gete, and the ordre and
dyssyplyne of knyghthode walketh at large wythowt ordre
ayenst the fyrst ordenaunce of knyghthode and the honorable
yn that behalfe. Touchynge the peryl of the ordre men may 35
eesely see by what penvrye and lakke of vertu oure eldres haue

2 to] om. N   7 translated] om. N   8 theym] J them N theyn S
10 they] om. J   16 of] om. J   24 connyng ys] connynges J   25 feede]
feele S fele NJ   33 knyghthode] knyghtly ordynaunce N   34 ayenst]
om. N

fallen from honoure, estate and dygnyte, and yn lyke wyse we
ben voyde yn vertu as they were or more, to iuge the state of
oure comon wele, for to stonde stable ys nowadayes called
wodenes and no reson. I haue redde how Phylostrate, oon of
the nobles of Grece, wepte whan he ha[r]d that famous and 5
excellent oratour of Roome called Tullyus, whyche yn eloquence exceded the Grekes and was neuyr seen aforetyme
of no Romeyne. And therfor they that loue the goodenes of
the comon wele may not to pytuously bewayle the dyscresyng
of the same and the vertu therof, for vertu hath the ymperyal 10
souereynte and yt allone maketh seure and happy peple, but
wykked and vnrightwys empyres and regnes ar neuyr longe
kept. Whatsomeuyr ys strengthed yn vertu ys ferme and sure,
and they that wyl lyve free wythowte bondage or confucion
let hem serue and obeye to reson and vertu. Now y make an 15
ende of my seyenge. Yf vertu flee from vs rvyne poursueth vs.

THE FREENDE

Thou hast ryght wele schewed the causes of oure wretched-
nes. But oon thyng y wayted aftyr, that thou / schuldest f. 47ᵛ
dessende fro the generalte to the more specyalte, and y pray 20
the wyth a feruent desyre that þou schewe me more effectuously what ys the roote of so grete euyl yn þe comon wele.

THE FELAW

Thou mayst see yn holy scripture that couetyse ys the roote
of alle euylles vnder the whyche honger of rychesse, ambycion 25
of power and myght ben closed.

THE FREENDE

I knowe wele þat auaryce ys a sercher of secrete wynnyng
and a moste desyrous swolow neyther happy to the very
fruyte of hauynge but feruently sette vppon the cursyd 30
appetyte of getyng. Ambycyone also y haue knowen whyche
desyreth chaungable glory and honours vndeserued whyche
wyth hys pompe and pryde brengeth yn rvyne. He norischeth

---

5 the] *om.* N   hard] N had SJ   8 loue] had lufe to N   9 bewayle] be
wayled N   dyscresyng] disincresyng N   11 seure] serue J   13 ferme]?
forme J   16 poursueth vs] foloweth after N   18 ryght] *om.* N
22 what] it *add.* N   30 sette] all *add.* N   30-1 the . . . of] *om.* N

envy and ys euer contrary to devyne thynges and to suche as
lyue yn prosperite. Also yn the most iust empyres we haue
somtyme founde euyl men gylty of ambycion and corrupte
wyth avaryce. These vyces ar annexed to kyngdoms and
empyres that prudence and wysedom ys wythdrawen from, 5
suche as schulde be counseylours for the comon wele, and
nowadayes we stande vnder the same forme, as ho seythe
vyces regne stylle and the same pestylence hath euyr warre
wyth hygh empyres and governaunces, and therfor they must
be ouercom and conquered.   10

THE FELAW

Thou spekest of a thyng to be done but not of hym that
schulde be the doer.

THE FREENDE

The delygence and wysedome of offycers and counseylours 15
ys that they ought represse the vyces whyche oppresse the
comon wele.

THE FELAW

Trouest thou not that yt ys an ynconvenyent thyng a man
that ys ouyrcome wyth couetyse may ouyrcome and rebelle 20
ayenst avaryce?

THE FREENDE

Thyr ben lawes whyche / reduce men by peyne and drede f. 4
vnto the ryght, whyche of malyce ar ayenst equyte.

THE FELAW   25

Lawe toke hys name somtyme of byndyng because that
men schulde be bownde to the lawe, but that ys the lawe where
equyte quykketh the lawes but vnequyte of the governour
mortefyeth the lawe. Yt ys holsom to the peple to be vnder a
ryghtwes lawe, but yt is moche more holsom to be governed 30
by a goode and a ryghtwes kynge, for they that governe the
comon wele of the goode thynges they make the best lawe and

---

3 men] *om*. N   4 kyngdoms] kyndoms N   9 governaunces] *sing*. N
24 the] *om*. N   26 name] of *add*. N   30 moche] *om*. J

they fulfyll the auctoryte of þe maker of the same lawe. Now
cometh to my mynde a party of the seurte and sadnes of the
lawes growndyd by the seyenge of the phylosophre named
Anaxagaras, whyche lykkened the lawes of men to coppe-
webbes whyche take and holde fast the smale flyes but the 5
grete flyes breke thorough the webbe and passe away lyghtly.
Lykewyse myghty men whyche vsurpe and take vppon
hemself lycence for to breke the lawe comaunde the pore men
to paye and suffre the penaunce of the lawe.

THE FREENDE 10

Yf yt be true that thou seyst, y merveyle gretely of the
vnschamefastnes of men.

THE FELAW

Yt apperyth opynly afore thyn yghen, for yt ys dayly yn vse.

THE FREENDE 15

Amonge tho thynges that ar wryte or taught of the comon
wele y holde thys fyrst for trewe, that no man ocupyeth the
souereynte by wey of offyce honestly but he come thyrto
ryghtwysly.

THE FELAW 20

Y iuge the same, for yt ys a scorneful thynge and a foule
spectacle to the comon wele yf men pollute wyth vyces sytte
yn hyghe offyces or estate as though thyr vyces schulde
opynly be schewed and / brought forthe yn syght of the f. 48ᵛ
peple. The freel and mevable comonte lyuen by ensample and 25
folowen the maneres and fortvne of myghty men, but they put
not theyre soules, lawes and ordenaunces made by com-
maundement so ryghtfully and wyth so grete reme[m]braunce
as they emprynte by ensample the lyuenge of theyr governour.
And therfor yf men yn estate hauynge governaunce be the 30
deffoulers of þer godlyhede they schulle be corrupters of
othyr mennes yntegryte and hole conuersacion. The lest man
þat synneth synneth to hymself, but they whos lyuenge ought
to be as ymage and ensample to othyr men, whan they synne
they synne to alle men. 35

1 maker . . . the (1)] om. N   34 as] an add. N

THE FREENDE

Al men desyre to take rewle yn the comon wele but fewe yn vertu, and therfor many attey(g)ne to rewle and governaunce of the comon wele wythoute vertu.

THE FELLAW   5

Whosomeuyr they be that take vppon hem the mageste wythoute vertu whatsomeuyr they fynde they seeke not the comon wele.

THE FREENDE

Yt may happe that a man may be gode and profytable to the 10 comon wele whyche pryvatly yn hys self ys vycyous.

THE FELLAW

The nature of goode thynges ys so ordeyned that no goode thynges dyscorde amonge hemself or sownde to euyl. Neuertheles euyl thynge may be contrary to euyl.   15

THE FREENDE

Of ryght yt ought to be graunted, but yt concludeth not necessarely that oon vertu folow vppon another. A man to be temporat it foloweth not of necessyte yn lyke wyse to be rightwis. Yt foloweth not though a man be ryghtwys that he 20 therfor haue the grete power of strengthe.

THE FELLAW

Thou avoydest couertly my sawes, but thou answer[s]t not to the / poynte. Thou hast lerned that to the trowthe of f. 49 an vnyuersal foloweth the trouthe of a pertyculer but not the 25 contrary. And therfor he that ys goode yn comovne y[s] goode yn pertyculer, and the ryght wey ys schewed to the comon wele by vertu, and therfor necessary yt ys that the offyce of vertu parteyne to the benyfyce of the wele publyke. Whyles a man ys not souereyne and mayster vppon hys owne passyons 30 and desyres how schal he mesure othyr mennes? Therfor by

---

11 hys self] hymself NJ   13–14 ys . . . thynges] *om.* J   18 folow]
foloweth N   19–20 of . . . not] *om.* J   21 haue] hath N   23 answerst]
answert SJ answers N   25 not] to *add.* N   26 ys (2)] J yn SN
27 to] yn J

the goode doctryne of oure fadres best and most comodyose
cyteseynes ar made of þe best men, and the most profytable
cyteseynes may be electe in most proved men by whose
governaunce the wele publyke may growe happy and more
fortu[n]atly perceuer and endure.   5

THE FREENDE

Yt ys a comon couerture of dedis and maneres and we vse yt
comonly that the wonderfull sownde of armes helpeth that
the lawes may not be had. Also the manyfolde plente of
vyces whyche ar done yn batayles suffreth not vertu to be   10
excercysed.

THE FELLAW

To hem that wyl synne or mysdo euery lytyl sterynge
yeueth occasyon, and therfor they that wyl not leve synne
s[e]che lesynges for coueryng of the same. Neuyrtheles lawes 15
ought more syngular[l]y to be kept whan they be ynpugned
wyth power of armes than at othyr sesons. Also vertu ought
more studyously to be encreced where yt ys so that batayles
ben medlyd wyth vyces, fore vertu schal neuyr schyne and
schewe ytself wythowte the apparence of hys contrary, for   20
connynge and vertu take theyre schewenge apparence abowte
thynges vnlyke to theym, for oon contrary nygh approchyng
to the thothyr is more strengthed yn hys apparaunce. And
therfor in batayles oure / eldres exemplefyed vnto vs most   f. 49ᵛ
scharpe and streyte lawes and most prykked sterynges and   25
yncytamentys of vertu. I wyl not speke yn how smale and lytel
thynges knyghtly doctryne hath iuged ryght grevous peynes
yn the whyche by grete provicion knyghthode come to grete
drede of vyces and synne.

THE FR[E]ENDE   30

I beseche the whylst the dygnite of the thyng and the
opportunyte of tyme accorde, forasmoche as thou hast spoken

1 best] J men *add*. SN   3 in] NJ *canc*. S   5 fortunatly] N forturatly
SJ   7 a] *om*. J   9 plente] plenteth N   10 whyche] *om*. N
batayles] *sing*. N   not] no N   15 seche] J suche S such N   16 syngularly]
N syngulary SJ   21 abowte] abought N   22 vnlyke] like N   23 the]
J the *add*. SN   25 sterynges] as *ins. above* S   30 Freende] Frrende S
31 thyng] ? kyng N

before of the best cyteseynes whyche ar (the) very preysed
and helpe of the comon wele, teche me whych thou callest
best cyteseynes and wurthy to haue governaunce of the
comon wele.

THE FELAW   5

He that wurschyppeth Go[d]dely thynges and setteth yn
mesure humayne thynges and yeueth hys delygence to
honeste, kepyng iustyce, and vnderstondeth that he ys not
borne for hymself but to þe comon wele, thys man y say ys
wurthy to be proferred to the governaunce of the comon wele. 10
Empyres and reemes stonde not by hemself, for alle power ys
of God, whyche knoweth euery mannes dede. To wurschip
any hevenly thyng, to make sacrefyces redolent wyth encence
or whosoeuyr constantly serues the mageste dyvyne schall
haue rewle and souereynte vppon othyr. Temporat and 15
vertuouse peple casteth no thyng hevely downe. The keper of
honeste ys bownden wyth no synfull lustes. The ryghtwys
man ys noyouse to nobody and delygent to euery mannes
wele, and he that yeueth hys mynde and ys soule to the charge
of the comon wele, not hauynge yn hymself pryvat affeccion, 20
scheweth hymself a man vnyuersal and ys not made oon man
but vnyuersal yn al men.

THE FREENDE

Thou hast wel spoken of the maners of goode men to the
comon wele, but yet I beseche the lete vs abyde awhyle lenger 25
yn the charge of the / sayde comon wele, for to knowe yt ys   f. 50
goode to a man and yt ys dylectable to serche yt. Sey therfor, y
prey the, yn what maner thynges schall the werkes appere yn
hem that louen the comon wele?

THE FELLAW   30

Yf they study to encrece the goodes of the cuntrey and
hemself suffre trouble for the same. They were ryght happy

---

2 and] the add. N   callest] the add. N   6 Goddely] J godly N goodely S
8 honeste] and add. N   kepyng] of add. N   9 for hymself] om. N
10 proferred] preferred N   13 sacrefyces] sing. N   14 whosoeuyr] whosomeuer J whoeuer N   17 honeste] honest J   21 made] J two letters canc.
after made S as add. N   28 werkes] sing. N

men that we remembred before that sought dethe for the lyfe
and the wele publyke and yn the dethe of o man procured the
lyfe of many men.

THE FREENDE

That ys a ful hard werke and a vertu ryght seldom vsed, for 5
yt ys naturelly yeuen to euery man of hys byrthe to kepe the
sweete lyff as longe as he may.

THE FELLAW

Thyr may neuer be ynoughe yeven to oure contre and
oure parentes, for of thy contre and thy parentes thou hast 10
taken thy lyffe and for hem thou owest thy lyfe. þou art more
streytely bounde to the peryle of thy lyfe for to kepe yt for
because that thorough thy labours the comon wele by the may
be the lenger kepte yn felycyte. By thys lawe batayles ar
leeful. Lyfe ys the comon wele and thys maner of dethe that 15
we flee oure fadres callyd yt a gloryous dethe.

THE FREENDE

Thys is a straunge thynge to oure maners as men lyue
nowadayes, for they speke and we desyre to lyue longe,
wherefor we ought most comonly speke of suche thynges as 20
may be done for the comon wele, sauynge oure lyff.

THE FELLAW

He lyueth vnhappely that redemeth hys lyfe wyth the
comon harme, for honest dethe hathe made more blessed and
gloryous men than foule lyfe.   25

THE FREENDE

Thyr ys not lyke maners of men nor lyke wytte as was
somtyme. Thys present age hath yeuen othyr maner of soules
and desyreth othyr maner of doctryne, and therfor yt ys
behoueful to speke of suche thynges as may be execute yn 30
dede.

---

2 o] a N   11 and . . . lyfe] *om*. N   15 thys] thu N   23 hys] *om*. N
27 not] no J   30 of] to N

THE FELLAW

Whereto than wylt thou haue me to say that þou wylt not here?

THE FREENDE

Y wulde knowe yn what thynge the vertu of man most 5 clerely / appereth to the comon wele bysyde the hurtyng of f. 5⁰ hys lyfe.

THE FELLAW

Thou sechest outwarde fortvne and y schal satyffye the wyth outewarde goode. I calle hym a goode man to the comon 10 wele, aftyr the consideracion of thys age, whyche ys streyte to hymself thorough whyche the comon wele may be more ample and more enlarged.

THE FREENDE

Thys secte hath but fewe dyssyples.   15

THE FELLAW

Hyt hath had many doctours and ther hathe ben whyche haue wythdrawe from theyr owne encrese, there owne synguler encrece, to ample and encrece the comon profyte. Many haue dyspysed the encrece of thyr owne house to 20 eschewe the detryment and hurte of the comon wele. Take hede of Valery, whyche was sette yn grete offyces and borne vp wyth the comon goodes, but for fere that he schulde haue made the comons bere to grete charges vppon hym wyth-drough and amynused hys householde and abated the pareyles 25 longynge to the same and alle for the comon wele. Yf thou wylt haue ensample of glorye nerre ayoyned to vertu thou mayst rede of that grete vertuous man named Fabyus, whych for hys grete merytes was called to the grettest offyce by the whyche he was made consule of Roome, whose sone aftyr the 30

2 Whereto] Wherefore J   9 satyffye] satysfye NJ   12 more] om. J
15 but] om. J   17 had] ? ihaue N   and . . . ben] and canc. whiche
hathe bene N and they hath ben J et fuere L   19 comon] wele and add. N
20 house] howses J   24 comons] to add. N   charges] sing. N   hym]
om. J   24-5 wythdrough] withdrowe N withdrawghe J   amynused]
mynused N   25 pareyles] parele J appareyls N

tyme of avoydaunce of the same offyce, for hys grete vertu by
electyon of the cyte was called to the same offyce, whyche hys
fader wulde not haue suffred lest that hys house by manyfolde
encrece of offycers schulde excede othyr yn honour and
rewarde to the charge of the comon wele of the cyte.   5

THE FREENDE

Thou schewest ferre and wonderful thynges to oure
Frenschemen and thou chefly denyest that þat they chefly
desyre.

THE FELLAW   10

They wyl not do that they chefly ought to do, for loke how
moche more / a man taketh vppon hym yn charge of the f. 51
comon wele, so moche more he oweth.

THE FREENDE

The ambycyous desyre of man stereth the soules of hem   15
wyth so grete swetnes as though yt naturally claue to the
bones of theym. Euery man desyreth gretter thynges to
hymself than to othyr men.

THE FELLAW

No goode man oughte to trust to suche synguler weles as   20
may be hurte to the comon wele.

THE FREENDE

Lyke as maners of men be, so ben theyre oppynyons,
wenyng whan they be wel at eese the comon wele ys not euyl
at eese.   25

THE FELLAW

But y beleue þe contrary, for whereas the comon wele ys
euyl at ese ther may no man be wele at eese. Who syttyng yn
estate precyously arrayde yn purpyl and fulfylled wyth
delycates festes, esed and molyfyed yn hys soule wyth   30
armonye and musycal swetnes, may calle hymself happy or
ioyfull syttyng yn a house for lak of sustynaunce lyke to

---

1 of (2)] had N   2 whyche] that *add*. J   3 fader] *om*. J   lest] lesse N
24 ys] it N   32 ioyfull] hoyfull J

oppresse hym to the dethe? What honoure or felycyte schall
be seure to the yf thy contre peryscheth? Thou wylt say that
many folke wolde. The seurte of [the] comon wele ys seen to
in euery syde, but the trust of oure pryvate wele ys yn
oureself, and therfor whyles we haue tyme we must see thyrto, 5
and comonly yt ys seyde lete vs vse prosperous fortvne whyles
we may.

THE FREENDE

Yf yt profyte to agaynesey the, whoso taketh oure rychesse,
oure honours or oure offyces from vs they take away oure lyfe 10
from vs.

THE FELLAW

Thou knowlegest alle thynges to by governed by fortvne
and alle affectuouse desyres of men and not by reson.

THE FREENDE   15

The nombre of men haue so ordeyned thyr lyfe and yt / f. 51ᵛ
ys so that they lawde and preyse a grete and an anymose werke
and they ioye yn the processe and parfourmynge of the same.

THE FELLAW

The sentence of the tragedy ys trewe: Prosperouse and 20
happy mysguydynge ys called vertu, but no man may wyth
hys seurte offre hymself to suche peryles, for no man gothe
oft a trobelous way but somtyme he fyndeth a falle.

THE FREENDE

Lete neuyr veyn and dysseytful glory presume to promyse 25
for to kepe seure, lyke as he wolde commaunde fortvne, that
þat vanyschethe awey vnder þe schynenge of freel and feyned
honour.

THE FELLAW

Yat at the leste lete the rvyne of theym that ben past be a 30
myrrour and feere to theym whom thys present veyn glory
desseyueth.

1 or] and N   3 ys] be N   10 away oure lyfe] oure life away N
18 they] the J

THE FREENDE

Thyr ys no seurte preuyded for thynges to come and thyr ys
grete forȝetylnes of thynges past. Yf thys present day passe
seurely and the next day succede than we thenke that we haue
ouyrcome fortvne. 5

THE FELLAW

Trustest thou to þe offyce of wysedom?

THE FREENDE

Certeynly yt ys seyde and as ho seyth openly preched that
yt ys wysedom yn thys dayes so to do that men may passe 10
wyth the tyme and lyue with the tyme.

THE FELLAW

Let hym bewarre how the tyme passe hem for he gothe not
ryght that seeth not hys wey befor hym, and he that
consydereth not the pathes of þe re[s]ydue of hys iourney 15
schal suffre som offence theryn, for the ende / and con- f. 52
clusyon of euery thynge to drede ys grete wysedome.

THE FREENDE

Men of dyuers condicions fynde dyuers kynde of lyueng,
and so the maners and the lawes of men aftyr þe dyuersyte of 20
the plages of the eyre ar varyed and chaunged, and so wyth
dyuerce tyme dyuerce lyff.

THE FELLAW

Tymes passen, fortvnes ar comon, and entremedlyd men ar
altred and chaunged, but that dyrectryce and chaare of 25
vertus and medyatryce of al thynges, that ys to say prudence,
abydeth vnmevable, euyr the same eternally, vnmesured, of a
Godely power wythowte whyche thyr may be no substaunce
nor abydyng yn thynges humayne, and though sche be
dyfferenced yn dyuerce men yet yn herselfe sche remayneth 30
hoole.

9 Certeynly] certeun N   ho] he N   preched] precheth N   10 thys] theis
N   13 hem] hym *canc*. hem S   15 resydue] N resedue J ? refydue S
25 dyrectryce] directorye N   28 Godely] goodly N   29 be] *om*. N

THE FREENDE

Thou hast dyscryved the olde wysedom, but we haue founde a newe. The wysedom maketh evyn the affectyons of man to the qualyte of þe thynge and the mesure of goode, but oure wysedom yn contrary wyse mesureth the thynges and 5 the ende of hem aftyr oure desyres.

THE FELLAW

That ys a dysseytefull, a freel and a feyned subtylte whyche thou callest wysedom. Sche by her ygnoraunce and euyl crafte brengeth man to most foule dethe. By her weyes 10 wykked men entre ynto the halles of kynges, and the same whan sche forsaketh hem sche plungeth and casteth hem ynto the profounde prysons of derknes. Sche makes the degrees by the whyche men ascende to horryble spectacles and to the axes of the executours of mortal iugement, whose exaltacion 15 ys a castyng downe and thyr wurschyp begynneth of rvyne. Most vsed / ende to the euyl dysposed comonte ys vnhonest f. 52ᵛ dethe.

THE FREENDE

I prey the, yf thou be not agrucched wyth my longe 20 taryenge, that thou woldest assoyle me a questyon.

THE FELLAW

I haue not Goddes power that I may answer to alle thynge.

THE FREENDE

Although thou mayst not telle me aftyr that dyffyculte as 25 my questyon requereth, yet answer me aftyr as thy faculte and power suffyseth.

THE FELLAW

Graunted yt ys to alle wyse and taught men to teche and to alle othyr to sey theyr oppynyon.   30

THE FREENDE

I desyre no iugement but dysputacion.

2 haue] a N   10 brengeth] a add. N   11 men] om. J   29 Graunted]
Graunte N

THE FELLAW

Sey whereyn thou doutest, and y schalle telle the as I feele.

THE FREENDE

Me semes that kyngdomes adioynyng vnto vs labour and be
enfecte wyth lyke vyces and men ouyral malygne yn vices and 5
euyl craftes, and yet they be not scourged wyth lyke peyne nor
haue demonstracions of lyk rvyne. Therfor yf thou haue
seyde trewe before, why do not lyke turmentes and peynes
onswer to lyke synne?

THE FELLAW
10

Let God iuge what ys done ayenste straungeres and
foreynes and let vs iuge as we feele.

THE FREENDE

Yet the fame renneth and we here alle day of othyr mennes
synnes, and yet we vnderstonde that they prospere. 15

THE FELLAW

Thou puttest thy mouthe ynto heuene and enforsest thyself
to consume the see wyth a schelle whan þou streynest of the
iugementes of the vnmesured Godhede, for oftentyme He
avaunseth a man that He may depresse; He lyfteth wykked 20
men on heyght to caste hem hedely downe ynto grete depnes;
He suffreth hem to prospere that He may more iustly ley to
hem her dyffautes; He purgeth the erthe of euyl men wyth
Hys pestylence [and] batayles. / f. 53

THE FREENDE
25

But many goode men perysche wyth the euyl men.

THE FELLAW

They that deyen yn theyre iustyce lyue yn eternyte.

THE FREENDE

Yf only wykked men were take awey, the devyne iustyce 30
schulde þe more clerely appere.

4 kyngdomes] kyndoms N   5 enfecte] effecte N   18 streynest] freynest J
24 and] *om.* SNJ et L   31 þe] *om.* N

THE FELLAW

Knowest thou not that He hydeth Hys secrete iugementes
fro men and hath made hem as a grete depnes that they may
and schal be derke and hydde fro man? For yt ys seldom seyn
by the yghen of (a) man that he see bothe the synne regnyng 5
and the peyne of the synne togedre, for he that seeth synners
yn here glorye and ryghtwys men yn her peyne paraventure
taketh hem wyth dethe before that they schul not inow see the
pvnyssyon of the synners nor the rewarde of ryghtwes men.
God procedeth softly to vengaunce, and He ys a dyssymelour 10
yn rewardyng of iustice, for He abydeth the repentaunce of
synners and He preveth by longe tyme the constaunce of
ryghtwys men, but yn open offences God reyseth a comon
scourge. Some He sleethe bycause of thyr opyn trespasse,
some bycause they wulde not wythstonde open offences. The 15
synners somtyme He taketh hem owt of the worlde yn con-
trycion of her synnes lest and they lyued lenger schulde
putrefye and falle agayn ynto corrupcion. He chastyseth hem
that folowen iustyce, not pvnyschyng theyr synne whyche
ys lytel or non but for to warne hem before to eschewe the 20
occasyons of synne. The leche cureth oftetymes the seeke
man yn purgynge the corrupte hvmours and draweth owte
also the goode humours, and oftentymes also he maketh the
pacyent feble to thentent that aftyrwarde that he may refourme hym to a newe strengthe. Yf God yn Hys mynde 25
dyvyne thenke vppon / kyngdomes anythyng He leueys man   f. 53ᵛ
vnknowyng therof, and ygnoraunte men eete and drynke and
ioye yn ther prosperyte and peese and sodeynly beholde and
thou schalt see how sodeynly cometh vppon hem the yre
of God and the euylles whyche they see not before. Wherto 30
arguest thou therfore by the ensample of foreyn and straunge
kyngdomes, how be yt I beleue hem nothynge further from
al ordre of vertu than we be, yet whatsomeuer they be He
ys the same God whiche scourged and pvnyscheth vs and
suffreth hem that they falle not, but whan the tyme of Hys 35

---

2 secrete] iustice and *add*. N   8 schul] schulde NJ   13 ryghtwys] rythwys
N   17 synnes] synners N   18 putrefye] putryfied N   19 folowen]
his *add. ins*. J   21 synne] synns N   26 kyngdomes] kyndoms N   leueys]
levys N   27 ygnoraunte] ignorance N   34 scourged] scourgeth N

vysytacion schal come and they haue synned agaynst Hym,
and He wythdrawe the arme of Hys dyffence and suffraunce
from theyme, than schal they be lyke vs. But the tyme and
momentes of the secrete iugementys of God ar yn the power
or þe Fadyr celestyal, and therfor yt sytteth not vs to knowe 5
or s[e]rche theym.

THE FREENDE

Oure fadyrs haue synned and haue be scourged betymes,
and yet haue they not be brought to rvyne of whych thou
spakest of lamentably yn the begynnyng.   10

THE FELLAW

They turned from her synne and God had of hem pyte, but
we wex olde yn oure synnes and we haue caste owt penaunce
owte of oure hertys, for ther ys no schame yn oure forhede,
and therfor paraventure God hath caste vs from the favour of 15
Hys face and hath turned away Hys yghen that oure sorow
and lamentacyon may not entre yn theym. Beholde thou how
oure Lorde somtyme chese to Hym the people of the Iues as a
verray specyal people before othyr and gaf hem Hys blessyng
above alle people and aftyrward gracyously many tymes 20
forgaff / theyre inyquytes and synnes, and at the last for ther f. 54
hard hertes He repentyd and forsoke theym that they schulde
perysche yn theyre newe invencions, and now they wander
vppon the face of the erthe yn servytute and bondage. We
then that haue receyued gretter thynges of the honde of God 25
before othyr Crysten people, yf we vnkyndely set apart the
feere of God we iuge oureself wurthy to haue more rygorous
punyschement.

THE FREENDE

Who schall be so prowde or so ouertrustyng vnto hymself 30
that he dredeth not God?

THE FELLAW

How schulde we beholde suche thynges as we dyspyse and
wyl not knowe?

6 serche] NJ sorche S   15 caste] *om.* N   16 sorow] soroure J
17 thou] *om.* N   18 the (2)] *om.* N   27 iuge] oure iuge *add.* N

THE FREENDE

Who but he that ys owte of mynde may be ygnoraunt of
God of whom we meve, we lyf and we are. By faythe, drede
and the grace of God the troone of oure nobles beforetyme
toke hys grounde and foundement of Crysten relygion 5
obserued and kept whych hath confermed the same to theyre
heyres. Let Clodryk, Clotayre, Dagobet, Pypyn and Charlemayn ber wytnes of trowthe yn thys mater, whyche exceded
othyr kynges wyth fayth and devocyon and deserued to be
made hygher yn empyre and souereyn mageste. Hyt was the 10
oppynyon and sentence of olde men that empyres and
souereyn governaunce yn reemes ys lightly holden and kept
aftyr the meenes of the fyrst getynge. Hyt ys also defycel and
harde to reteyn and kepe a reeme yf we entende to contrary
craftes and dysposycions.   15

THE FELLAW

Oure former princes honoured and wurschypped Hym
whom we knawe not, and therfor not wythoute cause hyt may
be dred lest the sentence of the Apostyl fall vppon vs, whyche
ys thys: forasmoche as they haue not labored to haue God 20
ynto ther knowlyge / God hath delyuered theym ynto wronge f. 54
and reproved vnderstondyng and wytt and blynded ther
sence and felyng.

THE FREENDE

Paraventure we chastysed schall turne and knowe Hym, 25
and He schall foryeven vs, for ofttymes vexsacion yeueth
vnderstandyng.

THE FELLAW

Byholde how theyr regnes vppon vs a grete plage and
horryble destruccion of batayl. We flee Hym and we turne 30
not to the Smyter that He may haue mercy vppon vs and sece
Hys hande.

THE FREENDE

I trowe He schal yeve peece aftyr thees woundes, and we

---

14 and kepe] *om.* N   22 reproved] *þair add.* N   24 Freende] Felaw N
28 Fellaw] Freend N   30 we] *om.* N   33 Freende] Felaw N

schall knawe that He ys mercyful and that He schal not
rewarde vs aftyr oure wykkednes but schall save vs vndyr the
multytude of Hys grete mercy so that we may knawe that the
helth of man ys veyn.

5

Wolde God that deth were prolonged fro me to the tyme
that vnknawen peece come from heven. Yf yt be longe from
vs, I aske thys fyrst of God, that thys day be my last day and
that I abyde not for to see that I haue forthought yn my
meditacion. The werynesse of batayle ys the incytyng and 10
occasyon of peece, and the wastyng of contrayes and grete
slaughtyr of men as wageth batayles, lyke as men wythdrawe
the mater of fyre to extynte and qwench the flambe therof.

Yf we haue dredful batayles let vs fyrst drede and hate the 15
fomentes and noryschyng of batayles.

[THE FELLAW]

Batayles ar not meved for theymself but for the concupyscence and desyres of man whych, yef they be repressed, the
batayles must be repressed of necessyte.   20

Hyt ys yn the mowthe of alle men that on bothe sydes of the
feyghters peece ys desyred.

Who wyl denye the name of peece whyche ys so swete that 25
no/thyng soundes swetter yn erthe? But thys ys of a dowble f. 55
vnderstandyng, for thynges ofttymes that acorde yn the name
dyscorde yn dede.

That ys certayn. But I meene that they desyre peece bothe 30
yn worde and dede.

5 Fellaw] Freend N   9 haue] *om.* N   11 contrayes] contraries N
13 extynte] extyncte N   14 Freende] Felaw N   17 The Fellaw] *ins.* J
om. SN   26 of] *om.* N   27 that] *om.* N   28 yn] the *add.* N

THE FELLAW

It ys the devyne spiracle and wyl of God that the comon peece and vnyuersal tranquyllyte be asked and desyred of ordynat sawles acordyng yn god.

THE FREENDE

And so yt ys also the comon gladnesse of þe people.

THE FELLAW

The beleue and credulyte of a comonte ys vncerteyn and vnstable whose sawles newe tydynges make vnstable, and the iugement of the comon ys chaungeable wyth fortune.

THE FREENDE

Among grete men and estates hyt ys so sayde, and the fame descendeth from them vnto the people.

THE FEELLAW

Belevyst thou not suche men to dysceyve and to be dysseyved whyche governe hygh palaces yn the whyche lesynges are noryschyd and brought furth?

THE FREENDE

The thyng self schal teche.

THE FELLAW

The grete and fervent desyre represseth hope. When I desyre a thyng more studyously, I abyde more feerfully.

THE FREENDE

Yf feyghters and bateylous men woolde haue peece schal hyt flee fro them?

THE FELLAW

I wote wele al men wolde haue peece to themself.

THE FREENDE

Let them haue hyt before.

---

2 spiracle] spracle N   6 comon] *om.* N   þe] comon *add.* N   8 credulyte]
crudelyte N   19 self] itself N   28 Freende] Felaw N

THE FELLAW

Let God avyce that, but peece be, I beseche God, to the kyngdam and the comon wele.

THE FREENDE

And they desyre yt and the pryvates desyre yt, let them 5 acorde togedyr and then yt schall be peece.

THE FELLAW

Thou makest a falce argument. /   f. 55ᵛ

THE FREENDE

Yt ys lytel to sey so but yf thou canst furnesch thy seyeng 10 wyt reason.

THE FELLAW

It ys an vnferme argument: I wolde peece and therfor I haue peece.

THE FREENDE   15

Thou þat knowest the vse of an argument, I pray the schewe yt me.

THE FELLAW

It ys clere and thou vnderstonde what ys peece.

THE FREENDE   20

I take yt after the comon vnderstandyng, but the more subtele vnderstondyng therof I abyde to knowe of the.

THE FELLAW

The ygnoraunce of peece maketh knawlege of myseryes. Whatsomeuyr they be that haue the peece of God and 25 dyspyce yt, they, as dystroyers of felycyte, afterward seke

1 Fellaw] Freende N   3 kyngdam] kyndam N   4 Freende] Felawe N
5 they] the J   7 Fellaw] Frende N   8 makest] mast N   9 Freende]
Felawe N   12 Fellaw] Frende N   15 Freende] Felaw N   18 Fellaw]
Freende N   20 Freende] Felaw N   21 comon vnderstandyng] tr. N
23 Fellaw] Freende N

wyth labour that they lost by sluggeschnes. It ys lyght to
styrre and meve batayles, but what ys order then to peece
theym? It ys a large way that ledeth to batayles, but yt ys an
angwysheous and strayte yssew oute therof. Therfor yt ys the
maner of wyse men yn tyme of peece to provyde batayles and 5
to be dred and to thenke that we must of necessyte suffre yn
batayle the yncomodites of þe same, whyche then we may not
eschewe by provicion for lakke of tyme. And for to vnder-
stande what peece ys by hys dyffenecion ys thus dyffynned:
Peece ys an ordynate tranquyllyte of sawle acordyng yn god. 10
And therfor whosomeuyr secheth ther owne profet and not of
the comon wele but studyen quyetly to reteyne goodes getyn
by ambycion and wythoute ynterrupcion to possede the
same, thes maner of people cryen peece to themself but yt ys 14
ther owne peece and not the / verray peece whych coun- f. 56
sayleth and conforteth sawles acordyng vnto god, whych
putteth togedyr the ordre of the comon weele yn armony by
deu proporcion. Peece ys the helth of the comon wele and a
dew havyour of the partes of the comonte togedere, and yt
perdureth yn helth as the body of man whan temperaunce ys 20
betwix the qualites and the humovrs and the armony of
proporcion whyche suffycyaunce calleth iustyce are served
convenyently to the compleccion. So the inco[lu]myte and
helth of the comon wele percevereth and endureth yf syngler
partes holde a lawful ordre to the goodes vnyuersall and yeff 25
non presume to vsurpe the place or the offyce of another. Of
verrey ryght the partyculer sawles schulde acorde vnto the
vnyuersall wele, and whenne that ys pryncypally entended by
hyt, it ys lyghtly comon to goodes partyculere.

THE FREENDE   30

Thou schalt satyffye me wyth one wurde yeff thou schewe
that when the comon wele ys made by the partyculer wele,
why ys it not then [the] ryght way [to] go to the comon wele by
desyre of goodes partyculer?

1 they] the N   5 provyde] for *add*. N   9 what] that J   21 humovrs]
humorvs J   23 incolumyte] incovymyte SNJ incolumis L   24 syngler]
synguler J   30 Freende] Felaw N   31 satyffye] satysfye NJ   33 ys]
? it N   the] N *om*. SJ   to] N *om*. SJ

THE FELLAW

Thou makest a falce argument for lakke of knowlyche of thy princyplees. Of the partyculer goode ordeyned to the comon goode ryseth the comon wele. Yf they be ordeyned to yt, necessary yt ys that the comon wele procede and be fyrst yn 5 the entent and that desyre of goode private folowe as partener of the comon wele.

THE FREENDE

Thou hast fulfylled my sawle, and thou hast as a man lerned dysputed and determyned of that thyng. 10

THE FELLAW

The varyable mutacion of fortune trowbleth to sore my mynde, whych ys not covenable to the peece that thou prechest.

THE FREENDE 15

Peece ys of so / grete perfeccion that yt acordeth to alle f. 56ᵛ men and to euery tyme and euery fortune. Whatsoeuer schall towche hym schall savoure part of hys mansuetude as redolent and swete smellyng myrre, by whos towche onely thyngys entermedled wyth hym schall haue swete savour. 20

THE FELLAW

It ys one thyng to gyf peece and to resseyve yt ys anothyr, but, whosomever gyffeth or taketh, hyt ys the grettest thyng of alle for to haue yt.

THE FREENDE 25

Y can spede a man that yt may be hadde, but the maner of havyng ys dyffycle and harde, but the thynges, the tyme and the manere schall schewe yt, for peece ys profytable to the ouyrcomer and necessary also to hym that ys ouyrcome. The

---

1 Fellaw] Frende N   4 goode] N good add. SJ   8 Freende] Felaw N
11 Fellaw] Frende N   15 Freende] Felawe N   20 haue . . . savour]
savoure swete N   21 Fellaw] Freende N   23 hyt] om. N   24 for]
om. N   haue] all add. ? canc. N   25 Freende] Felawe N   26 spede] anon
add. ? canc. N

ouyrcomer graunteth comodyously, and he that ys ouyrcome
asketh yt necessarely.

THE FELLAW

The ouyrcomers ben yn the better condicion, for they may
for ther owne desyre take and for the power of theyre 5
souereynte denye peece.

THE FREENDE

Thou knawest not the lawfull lawes of fortvne, for sche
oftentymes yeveth vyctory and yet sche denyeth pouer to vse
vyctory. Than schulde the ouyrcomers pry[n]cypally serche 10
peece whan choyse ys yn theyre owne honde. Fleeng vyctory
ys ofttymes the vndoyng of lordschyppes, for yt ys the pley
and dysporte of fortvne to subdewe the ouyrcomer to hym
that was ouyrcome. Thyr cometh to my mynde now the
oppynyon of that most wyse man Hamo of the noble cyte of 15
Cartage, whyche whan Hanybal, capteyne of the same, had
spoyled the Romeyns wyth many grevous batayles and leyde
seege to the cyte, made a requeste yn þe comon counseyle of
the seyde Cartage desyreng that legatys schulde be sent to
Roome to haue peece wyth hem seyeng, 'Now ys profyte to vs 20
to aske peece whyles power remayneth wyth vs / to graunte   f. 57
peece.' Hys request and counseyle was despysed, and after-
warde it fortuned yn contrarye that Cartage was by the
Roomeyns brent and vtterly dystroyed. Vyctorye lyth yn
dowte where he may remayne and ofttymes goten wyth grete 25
laboure ys kepped but schort space. Yn Perse here of ꝫerses,
that most myghty Duke of Perce, whyche was of so grete
puyssaunce that the multytude of hys schyppes shadowed the
see, the nombre of hys horses drynkyng made floodes drye,
whyche also brake the grete mownteynes and subdued the 30
see. The bregges were so ouyrcome thorough hys pryde that
vnnethe he escaped aloone yn a bote. Troye also, that grete
cyte brent by the Grekes, yave to theym a schort gladnes and a
wepable vyctorye, for they were sperpulyd ynto dyuers
londes and wedre-dryven by the sees that vnnethe of so grete 35
a nowmbre remayned the relyques, that ys to say the refuse.

---

3 Fellaw] Frende N   7 Freende] Felawe N   9 yeveth] the add. N
15 oppynyon] pl. N   26 here] om. N   31 hys pryde] tr. N

THE FELLAW

It ys a merveylous thyng yf victory be so ynconstaunt how
it ys holde so longe among oure enemyes.

THE FREENDE

Yf thou calle hyt vyctorye whych yeveth the ouyrcomers 5
and hem that be ouyrcomen angwysche and incomodytes.
Beleue thou me certeynly though they haue dystroyd the
contre, spoyled oure walled places and hath caste downe oure
batayles, yet so doyng they haue sufferd trowble, labour and 9
peyne. Oure lande ys oppressed wyth / armes, destytute of f. 57ᵛ
people and vertu, and yet theyre vyctory was so precyous that
yn the begynnyng they [f]ought with vs but wyth ten
thousand men.

THE FELLAW

It ys no force whether they ouercome vs with fewe or many 15
so they haue vyctory.

THE FREENDE

They are dayly consumed, and the maner of theyr victory
yeueth comforth þat we may trust wele of oureself.

THE FELLAW   20

Who may trust wele where the sawles be ouercomen and we
haue not hoope but only peece, whych ys yet yn dowte?

THE FREENDE

That þat ys to be done ys euer yn dowte tyl tyme that yt be
done.   25

THE FELLAW

Of wordes ys oppynyon, of the deede feythe.

THE FREENDE

It schal be do and thou schalt beleue yt.

1 Fellaw] Freende N   4 Freende] Felawe N   9 trowble, labour] tr. N
12 fought] J sought SN   13 men] om. J   14 Fellaw] Frende N
17 Freende] Felawe N   20 Fellaw] Freende N   22 not] no N
23 Freende] Felawe N   24 þat] om. N   26 Fellaw] Frende N
28 Freende] Felawe N   29 and] as N

THE FELLAW

After the thyng done, affyrmacion ys sure, but before yt ys dysseytfull.

THE FREENDE

Yf thyself wylt not beleve, suffre othyr to beleue.   5

THE FELLAW

Thou makest thynges certeyntees.

THE FREENDE

I reporte truly as yt ys sayde.

THE FELLAW   10

Thou folowest the worde, and I take heede of the deede.

THE FREENDE

Suffre me a lytel to reioyse myself yn the hoope of peece.

THE FELLAW

It ys a voyde hoope that ys redemyd wyth sorow, and I   15
woote how that the name of peece hath beguyled men.

THE FREENDE

Sey therfor why thou supposest to haue no peece.

THE FELLAW

But sey thou wheryn schal I parceyve peece whan no man   20
ys studyous for the pryncyples of peece?

THE FREENDE

A, thou art to harde and to scharpe.

THE FELLAW

Bewar lest thou be dysceyved wyth to alyght a beleve.   25

---

1 Fellaw] Frende N   4 Freende] Felawe N   6 Fellaw] Freende N
8 Freende] Felawe N   10 Fellaw] Freende N   11 Thou] Tho J Thu
N   12 Freende] Felaw N   14 Fellaw] Freende N   17 Freende]
Felawe N   19 Fellaw] Freende N   22 Freende] Felawe N
24 Fellaw] Freende N   25 to alyght a] a light N

THE FR[E]ENDE

I beseche the to let me haue yn knawlyge whych be the pry[n]cyples of peece.

THE FELLAW

Yf we schal cast away the maners whyche haue provokyd and caused / batayles. And yif we wolde holde and free theym we schall corrupte peece yef we haue any. Knawest thou not that iustyce ys the felaw of peece? For whyche wey that iustyce goth peece foloweth. Knowest not thou also (þat) yn partyculer desyres trouthe dyrectes iustyce. Thees bounden togeder by the lawe of dyvyne provydence neyther fortune may ouercome (ne) mannes power depart.

THE FREENDE

Ther are men that ar ful egal, for fortune of the tyme hath not take all [a]way. Let theym take the governaunce of the comon wele, and they by ther deede and example schal reduce other to an equale temperaunce of lyff.

THE FELLAW

Herde thou euer whate answer that noble man named Ma[n]lyus Torquatus gaue when þe cyte of Roome was corrupt yn maners and the cyte chase hym to þe consulat, chyef offyce of the same? He denyed and refused hyt, seyeng yn this wyse: 'Nayther I may bere nor suffre your maners nor ȝe myne empyre and soueraynte.' So paraventure may euery preved man to the governaunce of the wele publyke yn thys oure myserable tyme answer.

THE FREENDE

Wherefor than abyde we any lenger yssue or ende of this mater? Conclude thou thyself al these argumentes yn one wurde.

5

f. 58

10

15

20

25

30

---

1 Freende] J Frrende S Felawe N   4 Fellaw] Frende N   6 wolde] *perhaps canc.* S *om.* NJ   13 Freende] Felawe N   15 all away] N all way S alway J   18 Fellaw] Freende N   20 Manlyus] N Mawlyus SJ 22 hyt] þair N   24 So] *om.* J   27 Freende] Felawe N   29 these] *om.* N

THE FELLAW

I referre the sentence and the iugement vnto God, and as
He iugeth so be yt. Yf He wolde oure peece and the desyres of
man resyst and be contrary, He wyl schewe vs a plage and a
vengaunce. Of Hym aloone ys medycyne to [be] h[o]pped and 5
soght. Whatsomeuyr the wyttes of man laboreth, of God ys
the tranquyllite of reemes, and peece ys a celestyal and
hevenly gyft and ys as an ymage yn erthe of beatytude
celestyal. And therfor let oure disputacion seese. Let vs do
that semeth vs that we may schewe oureself wyth a clene 10
disposicion, portable of peece, bothe devowte of / hyt to be f. 58ᵛ
desyred and not vnkynde to receyve hyt.

THE FREENDE

I agre to the same iugement. Slepe calleth vs to quyete.
Farewel, broder. 15

THE FELLAW

And fare thou wele also. And fare we bothe wele yn the
comon peece. Amen.

Here endeth the famylyer dialogue of the frende and the
fellaw vppon the lamentable compleynt of the calamyte of 20
Fraunce.

1 Fellaw] Frende N   5 be] *om.* SNJ   hopped] o *unclear* S happed NJ
speranda L   9 do] *om.* N   11 portable] partable N   13 Freende]
Felawe N   16 Fellaw] Frende N

EXPLANATORY NOTES

*1/3** Freende*: SJ's *Auctour* may be the translation's original reading here. The Latin manuscripts have 'Amicus', but they all have 'ab Alano Auriga editus' after the title, 'Auriga' being the Latin equivalent of French 'charretier'.

1/11 Thyr . . . the: 'There is in thee'. This unusual spelling *thyr* does not appear in either *The Treatise of Hope* or *The Quadrilogue Invective*, but occurs frequently in the *Dialogue* as the demonstrative adverb and the third person plural possessive pronoun.

1/28-9 O . . . offyce: 'Cur Atropos festinas officium renitentis?' *hatest* may be a scribal error for *hastest*.

1/33 tragedye: Rosenthal notes that this refers to Seneca's *Hercules Furens*.

3/2 the . . . Varo: L. has 'illud Maronis'. Rosenthal could not locate the passage here in Virgil. The translator's *Varo* refers to Marcus Terentius Varro, whose writings include works on history and philosophy. *MED* has only one example of *hystoriagrafe* in the L. form *historiagraphus*.

3/24 Eutropolya: eutrapely (*MED* om., *OED* rare), 'pleasantness in conversation', is one of the seven moral virtues listed by Aristotle. Rosenthal glosses it as equivalent to L. 'urbanitas'.

7/12-19 Moreouer . . . wele: This is a very free translation of 'Praeterea ex Veteri Testamento signum habes, cum in offensione divini nominis aut legis suę blasphemia vestes abscindunt, quasi non solum ęgre iniuriam ferre, sed ob iniuriam publicam gravitate relicta insanire videautur.' There is no L. equivalent for *named doone*, and I have tried to make sense of the phrase by emending *doone* to *doome*. Rosenthal cites Genesis 44: 13, Numbers 14: 6, and Joshua 7: 6. The passage from Joshua seems to fit the context best.

10/12-13 merueylyously . . . herde: Given the structure here, the adverb *horrebely* is unusual. Perhaps an adjective has been scribally omitted.

13/8-10 for . . . apart: L. has 'Nam quocumque privatas copias in communem egestatem videris, ibi rei publicę nomen deletum est.' *and* in l. 10 may be a scribal error for *of*.

13/13-15 Wolde . . . folow: In L. these are the first words of the next speech of 'Amicus'.

13/26 returne . . . the: L. 'retorquebo'. Compare *The Treatise of Hope: retourne the argument ayeinst thiself*, 119/14.

14/15 Tyrence: In L. this allusion to Terence is omitted.

15/16 The Freende: In L. this speech is part of the preceding and following speeches of 'Sodalis' (*The Felaw*).

---

* References are to page and line numbers.

17/15 soules: Following this, the English omits the following passage from L.:

> Nos res et populos, simulque consilium amisimus miseri.
>
> AMICUS: Consilium forsitan ad tempus relinquimus, non amisimus, dum ad id revocata mente vertamur.
>
> SODALIS: Vanis coloribus duceris nec argumenti metam expectas.

18/4 hemself: Note the plural reference to *vertu*. Scribal error may be involved.

18/28 yt: i.e., all the evils noted above.

18/34-5 ayenst . . . behalfe: There is no L. equivalent here. The apparent use of *honorable* as a noun to mean 'what is honorable' is unusual and not recorded in *MED* or *OED*.

18/35-6; 19/1-4 Touchynge . . . reson: L. has 'Ex aliorum periculis nobis prospicere facile est, et qua virtutis penuria priores corruere, arbitrari nos stare dementia est.' Perhaps *ordre* is a scribal error.

20/27-9 but . . . lawe: Omission of part of L. creates a difficult reading here. L. has 'sed ut lex sit nunc, vix legisse satis erit. Princeps ipse animata lex est, cuius equitas leges vivificat, ac easdem mortificat regentis iniquitas.'

21/4 Anaxagaras: L. has 'Anacarsis', a more likely reference. Anacharsis, a Scythian, came to Athens about 594, where he became acquainted with Solon.

21/26-9 they . . . governour: L. has 'Nec instituta tam recte imprimunt edicto quam vita gubernantis exemplo.' The meaning of *put* is unclear in this free translation.

23/8 wonderfull: *OED* suggests the meanings 'disastrous', 'evil' only under the noun *wonder*, but compare *The Treatise of Hope*, 20/5.

24/16 hevely: This is perhaps a scribal error for *hevenly*. With the verb *casteth downe*, however, *hevely* is appropriate.

26/22 P. Valerius Publicola, one of a famous patrician family in Rome, played a prominent role in overthrowing the kings and was made consul in 509 BC, the first year of the republic. He and other members of his family were always strong advocates of the rights of the plebians and often proposed laws to allow the plebians more liberty.

26/27-30; 27/1-5 thou . . . cyte: See Livy, 22: 8, 44: 35 (Rosenthal). This passage is a good example of the free translation of the author: 'Fabium habes Maximum, consulem, qui oblatum filio consulatum repulit, ne eadem familia frequentia magistratus antecelleret.'

28/2-7 Thou . . . may: 'Amicus' says this in L., and the next speech of 'Sodalis', as well as the first part of the following speech of 'Amicus', is omitted in the English:

> SODALIS: Affectatam ignorantiam respondes. Qui enim sedes excelsas tenaciter cupideque servant, eas sepius improvide turpiterque perdunt.
>
> AMICUS: Respondent: Quod adversa feret fortuna, patiendum erit. Interim vero, dum prospera est, utamur, aiunt.

31/18 streynest of: *OED* does not give the meaning 'contend against' for this verb. Therefore, perhaps J's *freynest* ('inquire about') is the original reading.

35/14 ff. There is variance among the English manuscripts, as well as between the English and the Latin, from this point on in regard to the speakers. N, in variance with SJ, in this and the preceding four speeches assigns those of the 'Freende' to the 'Felaw' and vice versa. Then J assigns *35/18-20*, part of the preceding speech of the 'Freende' in S, to the 'Felaw'. This variance is interesting in that in the Latin, *35/10-13* (*The . . . therof*) is spoken by 'Amicus', and *35/15-16*, along with *35/18-20*, by 'Sodalis'. J's addition of *The Fellaw* at *35/17* may perhaps be just the scribe's addition to avoid having two speeches in a row assigned to the 'Freende'. Beginning at *36/28*, N reverses the speakers throughout the rest of the text. See also notes to *39/12-14*; *39/16-22*; *39/23-4*, and *39/26-7* for differences between the Latin and SJ.

36/4 god: It is unclear whether the author intended *God* or *good* here, although *good* would translate the Latin 'bonum' in the speech.

36/29 before: L. 'igitur'.

38/18-23 Peece . . . compleccion: This is a rather unclear translation of L. 'Est enim pax rei publicę sanitas et debita partium communitatis invicem habitudo. Et velut corpus humanum in sanitate perdurat, cum inter qualitates et humores temperamentum, quod adiustitiam medici vocant, et proportionis armonia complexion servatur. . . .'

39/2 knowlyche: Because of the repetition in L. of 'Ex particularibus', the following sentences were probably scribally omitted in the L. manuscript used by the translator: 'Ex particularibus enim bonis propter se acceptis nichil unum conficitur, quoniam contraria nulli unquam tertio conveniunt. Bona vero privata propter se quęsita contrarietates et bella faciunt, cum a diversis petantur quę unico competant.'

39/3 goode: *good* is probably added in error by dittography in SJ. Without it, as in N, the sentence follows the Latin structure exactly.

39/12-14 The . . . prechest: In L. these words are part of the preceding speech of 'Amicus'.

39/16-22 Peece . . . anothyr: In L. all of this is the next speech of 'Sodalis'.

39/23-4 but . . . yt: In L. this is the next speech of 'Amicus'.

39/26-7 Y . . . harde: In L. this is the next speech of 'Sodalis'. Then 'Amicus' has the rest of the speech.

40/8 lawfull: Perhaps this is a scribal error for *vnlawfull* since L. has 'illegitimas'.

43/5-6 Yf . . . batayles: This sentence is incomplete because the translation omits the L. main clause: 'hoc pacis fundamentum est'.

GLOSSARY

In accordance with EETS practice, *y* when it represents a vowel is treated as a variant of *i*; *i* when it represents a consonant has the place of modern *j*; *u* and *v* when they represent consonants have the place of *v*, and when they represent vowels the place of modern *u*; and ʒ is treated as *y* or *z*, whichever is appropriate. References are to page and line numbers. Usual verb forms are not recorded unless variant forms occur in the treatise. An asterisk beside a page/line reference indicates an editorial emendation not found in the English manuscripts.

abasched *ppl. adj.* afraid, upset *10/21*.

abaschynge *vbl. n.* ∼ *of any countenaunce* losing composure *4/17–18*.

abyde *pr. 1 sg.* wait *36/22, 37/22*. ∼ *yn* linger over, dwell upon *24/25–6*.

abydyng *vbl. n.* permanence *29/29*.

abowte *prep.* in the presence of *23/21*.

accheue *v.* satisfy *10/20*.

ac(c)orde *pr. pl.* are suitable *23/32*; agree *35/27*. ∼ *to (vnto)* be harmonious or compatible with *38/27, 39/16*. ∼ *togedyr* come to an agreement *37/6*. *acordyng yn (vnto) pr. p.* harmonious or compatible with *36/4, 38/16*. *ys accordyng to the same* agrees *12/29–30*.

adioyned *pp.* ∼ *to* united with *15/25*. *ayoyned to ppl. adj.* connected with *26/27*. *adioynyng vnto* adjacent to, near, *31/4*.

affeccion *n.* in *pryvat* ∼ self-love *24/20*.

affectuouse *adj.* well-disposed *28/14*.

affyrmacion *n.* assurance that something is true *42/2*.

after, aftyr *prep.* according to, in keeping with *15/9, 26/11, 34/13*. ∼ *as conj.* so far as *30/26*.

agaynesey *v.* contradict *28/9*.

age *n.* life *1/24. ronne yn* ∼ advanced in years *1/28*.

agrucched *pp.* ∼ *wyth* offended by *30/20*.

alyght *adj.* 'light' = careless; easily arrived at *42/25*.

alle day *adv.* again and again *31/14*.

amynused *pa. t.* reduced in size, value, etc. *26/25*.

ample *v.* increase *26/19* (*MED* v. om.; *OED* rare).

ample *adj.* abundant *26/13*.

anest *prep.* in the presence of *2/21*.

angwysheous *adj.* troubled *38/4*.

any more *adv.* further *17/5*.

anymose *adj.* courageous *28/17*.

anythyng *adv.* in any way at all *11/22, 32/26*.

applye *pr. pl.* strive *12/25*.

argvynge *vbl. n.* argument in support of a claim *17/3*.

armonye *n.* music *27/31*.

as(s)aye *v.* undertake *14/16*; *pr. pl.* *14/16*.

asseured *ppl. adj.* confident *18/15*.

assoyle *v.* answer *30/21*.

aswaged *pp.* appeased *16/5*.

at *prep.* in *18/31*.

at *conj.* that *4/30*.

attemp(e)raunce *n.* moderation *1/17, 15/4*.

avaunce *v.* help *16/11*.

avaunseth *pr. 3 sg.* promotes in rank or status *31/20*.

aventure *n.* event, accident *14/17*.

aventuryng *vbl. n.* rash and risky ventures *9/34* (*MED* om.; *OED* 1580).

avyce *v.* consider *37/2*.

avoydaunce *n.* vacancy *27/1*.

batayles *n. pl.* armies *41/9*.

bateylous *adj.* fond of fighting, warlike *36/24*.

be *v.* ~ *aboute* endeavour *12/5*.

behoueful *adj.* necessary *25/30*.

beleue *n.* faith, confidence *15/24*.

benyfyce *n.* benefit *22/29*.

betymes *adv.* at an early time *33/8*.

bynde *v.* pledge (oneself) *17/21*. **bounde** *pp.* committed *25/12*. **bownde** subject (to) *20/27*. *bownden wyth* dominated by *24/17*.

byndyng *vbl. n.* commitment, submission *20/26*.

bysyde *prep.* over and above *26/6*.

bodyes *n. pl.* physical aspects of people as opposed to spiritual aspects *16/27. celestyal* ~ stars *11/22*.

borne *pp.* ~ *vp wyth* supported by *26/22-3*.

brake *pa. t.* made way through *40/30*. ~ *owt* burst forth *7/2*. **broken** *pp.* destroyed *15/14*.

brede *n.* livelihood *11/24*.

bregges *n. pl.* bridges *40/31*.

called *pp.* ~ *for* considered *13/5*.

casteth *pr. 3 sg.* ~ *oute* forces out *15/21*. ~ *downe pr. pl.* reject *24/16; pp.* overcome *41/8*.

castyng *vbl. n.* ~ *downe* overthrowing *30/16*.

chaare *n.* charioteer *29/25* (*MED, OED* om.; L. 'auriga').

chalangeth *pr. 3 sg.* lays claim to *9/28*.

charge *n.* solicitous care *24/19*; burden (financial etc.) *27/5; pl.* expenses *26/24*. ~ *of* feeling of

concern for *24/26*. *in* ~ *of* at the expense of *27/12*.

chargeable *adj.* answerable, blameworthy *9/2* (*MED* meaning om.; *OED* 1546).

charged *pp.* burdened financially *1/16*.

chaunces *n. pl.* events *13/19*.

chaungable *adj.* transitory *19/32*.

chese *pa. t.* chose *33/18*; **chase** *43/21*.

clave *pa. t. subj.* stuck, adhered *27/16*.

clene *adj.* righteous *44/10*.

clerenes *n.* moral purity *16/30*.

closed *pp.* included *19/26*.

comforth *n.* encouragement *41/19*.

comodyose *adj.* useful *23/1* (*MED, OED* no ex. referring to people).

comodyously *adv.* profitably *40/1*.

comon *n.* common people *36/10. yn comovne* in general *22/26*.

comon *pp. in ys* ~ *to* reaches *38/29*.

comonte *n.* people of a nation *30/17, 36/8*; common people *21/25*.

compase *n. in yn* ~ all around *10/11*.

compleccion *n.* nature resulting from blending of the humours in varying proportions *38/23*.

composycion *n.* setting up and arranging *18/17*.

concludeth *pr. 3 sg.* proves *22/17*.

concupyscence *n.* worldly desires *35/18-19*.

condyte *v.* guide *14/11*; conduct, lead *1/21*.

condyteng *vbl. n.* managing, carrying on *9/10*.

confermed *pp.* strengthened *34/6*.

confounde *pr. pl.* confuse *10/17; pp.* destroyed *9/24*.

confucion *n.* ruin, destruction *19/14*.

coniecture *n.* scheming *13/13*.

conserueth *pr. 3 sg.* maintains in good order *15/11*.

constreyne *pr. pl.* restrict *15/22*; *pp.* prompted *16/21*.

consume *v.* empty, drink up *31/18* (*MED*, *OED* no use like this; L. 'exhaurire'); *pp.* slain *41/18*.

contrary *adj.* hostile *22/15*; immoral *34/14*.

conuenyently *adv.* appropriately, aptly *13/22*; properly *38/23*.

conuersacion *n.* way of life *21/32*.

convyct *ppl. adj.* defeated (in argument) *5/24*.

copy *n.* plenty *6/10*.

coppe-webbes *n. pl.* spiderwebs *21/4-5*.

couenable *adj.* proper *15/6*; reasonable *17/9*; favourable *39/13*.

coueryng *vbl. n.* concealing *23/15*.

couertly *adv.* ambiguously *22/23*.

couerture *n.* deceitful justification or defense (for conduct) *23/7* (*MED*, *OED* no ex. like this).

covnte *pr. 1 sg.* reckon, esteem (with obj. cl.) *10/32* (*MED* meaning om.; *OED* 1682).

countenaunce *n.* mode of behaviour *4/14*; see **abaschynge**.

craft(e) *n.* deceit *30/10*; *pl.* behaviour *10/24*, *31/6*, *34/15*. by ~ deceitfully *9/32*.

cryen *pr. pl.* demand *38/14*.

declyne *v.* turn aside *5/14*.

deffoulers *n. pl.* defilers (morally) *21/31*.

defycel *adj.* difficult *34/13*; **dyffycle** *39/27*.

delycacyes *n. pl.* luxuries, pleasures *15/3*.

delycates *adj. pl.* epicurean *27/30*.

delygence *n.* in *yeueth his* ~ pays attention, devotes himself (to) *24/7*.

delygent *adj.* ~ *to* heedful of *24/18*.

demerytes *n. pl.* sins *18/6*.

demonstracions *n. pl.* signs *31/7*.

denye *v.* refuse to believe in *35/25*.

depart *v.* separate *43/12*.

depnes *n.* deepness (suggesting Hell) *31/21*; mystery *32/3*.

depresse *v.* overthrow *31/20*.

derke *adj.* hard to understand *32/4*.

desereden *pa. t.* desired *10/1*.

desyrous *adj.* greedy *19/29*.

despyse *pr. pl.* refuse *14/12*. **dyspyce** scorn *37/26*. **despysed** *pp.* *40/22*. **dyspysed** disregarded (as unimportant) *26/20*.

dessende *v.* pass (from the general to the specific) *19/20*.

determyned *pp.* ~ *of* discussed, explained *39/10*.

devowte *adj.* ~ *of* dedicated to *44/11*.

dew(e) *adj.* proper, appropriate *10/25*, *18/17*; morally right *38/19*.

dyffautes *n. pl.* sins *31/23*.

dyfferenced *pp.* different *29/30*.

dylectable *adj.* intellectually delightful *24/27*.

dyrectryce *n.* female who directs or governs *29/25* (*MED* om.; *OED* 1631).

dyscorde *pr. pl.* disagree *22/14*, *35/28*.

dyscresyng *vbl. n.* diminution *19/9*.

dyscryved *pp.* explained *30/2*.

dysolate *adj.* miserable *18/10*.

dysporte *n.* sport, amusing activity *40/13*.

dysposycions *n. pl.* conditions *15/17*; intentions *34/15*.

dysputacion *n.* discussion *30/32*.

dysputed *pp.* ~ *of* discussed, explained *39/10*.

dyssesed *pp.* dispossessed unlawfully *9/37*.

dyssymelour *n.* dissembler *32/10*.

dyssolue *pr. pl. subj.* fig., destroy *15/3*.

do *v.* in *haue* ⌒ have done with it, hurry up *13/29*.

doctours *n. pl.* authorities *26/17*.

doome *n.* ? adverse fate; ? final death, destruction *7/14*.*

dowble *adj.* deceptive *35/26*.

drede *v.* fear *29/17*. **dradde** *pp.* *8/16*. **dred** afraid *38/6*.

drede *n.* fear *10/22*, *15/23*; deep awe or reverence *34/3*.

dulle *adj.* lethargic *12/24*.

durynge *vbl. n.* lastingness *16/31*.

dwellers *n. pl.* natives *7/27*.

eese *n.* wantonness *15/3*.

effectuously *adv.* truly, actually *19/21-2*.

egal *adj.* always the same *3/28*; fair, just *16/4, 43/14*.

egyrly *adv.* harshly *7/8*.

eyre *n.* atmosphere *29/21*.

empyre *n.* absolute rule or power *43/24*.

emprynte *pr. pl.* consider and re-member carefully *21/29*.

encrese *n.* income, revenue *26/18*.

ende *n.* final resolution *43/28*.

enfecte *pp.* polluted *31/5*.

enforsest *pr. 2 sg. refl.* strive *31/17*; **enforce** *pr. pl.* *11/22*.

enlarge *pr. pl. subj.* bestow liberally *15/7*; *pp.* endowed with bounti-ful gifts *26/13* (*MED* meaning om.).

entende *pr. pl.* be inclined to *34/14*.

entremedyl *v. refl.* be mixed *11/8* (*MED, OED* refl. om.). **entre-medlyd** *ppl. adj.* confused, mixed up *29/24* (*MED, OED* fig. meaning om.). **entermedled** mingled *39/20*.

estate *n.* in *yn* ⌒ of rank *21/30*; in a manner appropriate to high rank *27/29*; *pl.* high ranking people *36/12*.

euydently *adv.* unmistakably *13/13*.

euyn *adj.* steadfast *15/4*. *make* ⌒ ? put right *5/11* (L. 'equabit'). *maketh evyn* adjusts exactly *30/3*.

eutropolya *n.* 'pleasantness in con-versation' *3/24* (*MED* om.; *OED* rare; see note).

exaltacion *n.* supreme degree of power or fame *30/15*.

executour *n.* one who gives effect to *2/17* (*MED* om.; *OED* only one ex.); *pl.* those who carry into effect *30/15*.

experyence *n.* in *haue yn* ⌒ have experienced *9/12*.

expresse *pr. pl.* betoken *9/20*.

extynte *v.* extinguish *35/13* (**extyncte** N).

extorcions *n. pl.* acts of wresting possessions by force *10/10*.

fame *n.* rumour, report *31/14*, *36/12*.

feele *pr. l. sg.* understand *31/2*; *pr. pl.* *31/12*.

feerce *adj.* violent *6/4*.

feere *n.* object of fear *28/31*.

feyned *ppl. adj.* false *28/27*; deceit-ful *30/8*.

ferre *adj.* remote *27/7*.

fylthes *n. pl.* sins *8/30*.

fyndeth *pr. 3 sg.* experiences *28/23*.

fyrmament *n.* firm foundation *14/21*.

fleeng *ppl. adj.* transitory *40/11*.

floodes *n. pl.* rivers *40/29*.

floryschyng youthe *n. phr.* the bloom of youth *1/27* (*MED* om.; *OED* 1562).

folowest *pr. 2 sg.* accept *42/11*. *folow vppon pr. subj.* accompanies, results from *22/18*.

fomentes *n. pl.* stimuli, things that foment or encourage *35/16* (*MED* meaning om.; *OED* 1604).

force *n.* in *it ys no* ⌒ it is not important *41/15*.

foreynes *n. pl.* foreigners *31/11*.

forme *n.* in *vnder the same* ~ in the same condition *20/7*.

formefadyrs *n. pl.* forefathers *9/8*.

forthought *pp.* anticipated *35/9*.

fortunably *adv.* by fortune *13/18* (*MED* om.; *OED* only ex. 1555).

fortuned *pa. t.* happened *40/23*.

fortvnes *n. pl.* accidents *29/24*.

forӡetylnes *n.* forgetfulness *29/3*.

foundement *n.* basis *34/5*.

free *pr. subj.* release from constraint *43/6*.

freel *adj.* weak *15/30*, *18/23*; morally weak *9/14*.

fulfyll *pr. pl.* comply with *21/1* (**fulfuyll** J). **fulfylled** *ppl. adj.* glutted *27/29*.

furnesch *v.* support *37/10* (*MED*, *OED* meaning om.; L. 'sub-iunxeris').

generalte *n.* general *19/20*.

gentyles *n. pl.* knights, nobles *15/12*.

god *n.* good *36/4*, *38/10*, *38/16* (L. 'bonum', 'bono'). **goode(s) vnyuersall** welfare or benefit of all *38/25*. **goode(s) partyculer(e)** welfare or benefit of individuals *38/29*, *39/3*.

godlyhede *n.* virtue *21/31*.

goodenes *n.* prosperity *19/8*.

gothe *pr. 3 sg.* walks *28/22*.

gouernayle *n.* rudder *14/4*.

grevousnes *n.* mental pain *7/5*.

groce *adj.* dull, stupid *18/22* (*MED* meaning om.; *OED* 1526).

grounde *n.* basis *34/5*.

growndyd *ppl. adj.* established *21/3*.

halowes *n. pl.* saints *10/19*.

happe *v.* occur *22/10*; *pr. 3 sg.* chances *13/18*.

harde *adj.* oppressive *11/12*; painful *17/2*; unfeeling, severe *42/23*.

harde *adv.* firmly *11/4*.

hardynes(se) resolution, courage *7/7*; audacity, presumption *18/30*.

hasted *pa. t.* hastened *11/30*.

hath *pr. 3 sg.* ~ *warre* wages war *20/8*. **had** *pp.* kept *23/9*.

havyour *n.* behaviour *38/19*.

hedely *adv.* headlong, speedily *31/21*.

hedy *adj.* violent, rash *9/34*.

hedynes *n.* rashness, self-will *18/27*.

helth *n.* prosperity *35/4*.

heuely *adv.* with anger *7/16*, *24/16* (see note).

heuy *adj.* evil, dulled with sin *9/2*.

hevynes *n.* sorrow *17/10*.

hystoriagrafe *n.* historian *3/2* (*MED* 'historiagraphus'; *OED* om.).

hole *adj.* morally healthy *21/32*.

honest *adj.* honourable *25/24*.

honeste *n.* virtue *24/8*.

honorable ? *n.* what would be honourable *18/34* (*MED*, *OED* meaning om.; see note).

hopped *pp.* hoped for *44/5*.

hote *adj.* zealous *9/9*.

how *see* **more**.

how be yt *adv. conj.* notwithstanding that *32/32*.

humanyte *n.* human nature *16/27*.

hurte *adj.* injurious *27/21*.

iangler *n.* idle talker *3/27*.

iaper *n.* jester *3/27*.

ymages *n. pl.* statues *10/4*.

yn *prep.* in the hands of *12/11*, *28/4*; with *18/25*, *22/2*; among *23/3*; by means of *23/28*.

yncytamentys *n. pl.* incentives, stimuli *23/26* (*MED* om.; *OED* sp. om.; L. 'incitamenta').

incytyng *vbl. n.* instigation *35/10* (*MED* om.; *OED* vbl. n. 1611).

incolumyte *n.* safety *38/23***.

yncomodites *n. pl.* evils, misfortunes *38/7*, *41/6*.

ynconvenyent *adj*. absurd *20/19*.
yndyfferently *adv*. indiscrimin-
ately *10/14*.
ynfenyte *n*. in *by an* ⌣ for perpe-
tuity *8/25*.
ynpugned *pp*. opposed *23/16*.
yntegryte *n*. purity *21/32*.
invencion *n*. scheme *9/31*; *pl*.
33/23.
yrketh *pr. 3 sg*. wearies *11/7*.
yrksomnes *n*. loathing, pain *8/17*.
ys *pron. poss*. his *24/19*.
yssue *n*. decision about a matter
of controversy *43/28. yssew oute*
means of egress *38/4*.
iugement *n*. decisive opinion
30/32.
iust *adj*. illustrious *20/2*.

kepe *v*. continue *25/6*. **kepped** *pp*.
kept *40/26*.
keper *n*. possessor *24/16*.
kyt *pp*. torn to pieces *14/3*.
knowlyche *v*. acknowledge *6/2*.
knowlegest *pr. 2 sg*. claim *28/13*.
knowlyge *n*. in *haue ynto* ⌣ know
34/21. haue yn knawlyge 43/2.

labour *pr. pl*. are oppressed *31/4*.
laboreth *pr. pl*. endeavour to
bring about *44/6*. **labored** *pp*.
exerted themselves *34/20*.
large *n*. in *at* ⌣ without strictness
18/33.
large *adj*. broad, i.e., undisciplined
38/3.
largesse *n*. freedom to do what one
will *18/29* (*MED* meaning ques-
tioned; L. 'licentiẹ'; note also
lycence, l. 29).
le(e)ful *adj*. right, proper *10/23*,
25/15; permissible *17/5*.
ley *pr. 1 sg*. cite (an example) *4/12*.
⌣ *to v*. blame for *31/22*.
lesynges *n. pl*. lies, deceptions
23/15, 36/17.
lest *adj*. humblest *21/32*.

lettre *n*. written account *6/28*; *pl*.
learning *18/7*.
lettreture *n*. book learning *9/34*.
lyterature learning in general
17/25.
lyght *adj*. easy *38/1*; *see* **alyght**.
lyghtly *adv*. easily *21/6*.
lyke *adj*. likely *13/17*; similar *25/27*.
lyketh *pr. 3 sg*. pleases *10/22*.
lytel *adv*. too little *37/10*.
lyth *pr. 3 sg*. is *40/24*.
loke *imp*. ⌣ *how* however *27/11*.
⌣ *what wey that* wherever *18/3*.
longe *adj*. distant (in time) *35/7*.
longynge *ppl. adj*. ⌣ *to* charac-
teristic of *26/26*.

made *pp*. brought about *38/32*; *see*
euyn.
malygne *ppl. adj*. wicked *31/5*.
manaces *n. pl*. threats of potential
danger *13/19*.
maner(e) *n*. moral practice *18/8*;
pl. *24/24*; practices *18/19, 25/18.*
yn ⌣ so to speak *4/9*. ⌣ *and
mesure* limit *7/6-7*; *see* **ordre**.
manyfolde *adj*. many times mag-
nified *23/9*; great *27/3*.
mater *n*. timber, substance that
makes a fire burn *35/13*. ⌣ *of*
reason for *11/1*.
medyatryce *n*. one who brings
about peace *29/26*.
medyl *pr. pl*. mix *10/18*; *pp*. *9/34.*
⌣ *wyth* infused with *23/19*.
meene *n*. golden mean *3/27. by a
dewe* ⌣ properly *14/12*.
memoryal *n*. legacy *10/7*.
merveyle *n*. in *haue had* ⌣ have
been astonished *18/9*.
merveyle *pr. 1 sg*. ⌣ *of* am
astonished at *21/11*.
merveyl(y)ously *adv*. horribly
10/12; strangely *12/29*.
merveylous *adv*. exceedingly
18/16.
mesure *n*. extent, quantity *30/4.
by* ⌣ by due proportion *15/10*.

kepe ∼ be temperate or moderate *11/14. kepest no* ∼ *5/8. wyth- oute* ∼ immoderately *6/3; see* **maner(e), setteth**.

mesure *v.* adjust *4/9*; govern *22/31*; *pr. 3 sg.* judges *30/5. egally mesured ppl. adj.* impartial *15/10*.

mevable *adj.* tractable *21/25*.

meve *v.* incite *38/2*; *imp.* urge *11/1*; *pr. 1 sg. 12/13*; *pr. 2 sg.* speak, argue *12/10*; *pp.* aroused, angered *4/21*.

mevyng *vbl. n.* inclination, feeling *15/6*.

myrrour *n.* example of that which is to be avoided *28/31*.

mysguydynge *vbl. n.* evil be- haviour *28/21* (*MED* meaning om.).

moche *adj.* many *13/4*.

molyfyed *ppl. adj.* made soft, weakened *27/30*.

mortefyeth *pr. 3 sg.* destroys *20/ 29*.

mouthe *n.* in *puttest thy* ∼ *ynto heuene* challenge heaven with your words *31/17*.

multytude *n.* abundance *35/3*.

name *n.* renown, reputation *13/9* (see note). *yn the* ∼ nominally *35/27*.

named *pa. t.* invoked *7/14*.

natal dayes *n. phr.* birthdays *8/22*.

nature *n.* inherent characteristics (of man descended from Adam) *8/33*.

neyther *adv.* not *19/29*.

nerre *adv.* closer spiritually *26/27*.

nygh *adv.* thoroughly *12/15*; near *23/22*.

nobles ? *adj. pl.*, ? error for *sg.* noble *15/12*.

noyouse *adj.* harmful *24/18*.

nombre *n.* in *the* ∼ a large number *28/16*.

norischeth *pr. 3 sg.* fosters *19/33*;

pr. pl. produce *18/21*; *pp. 36/17*; encouraged *9/12*.

noryschyng *vbl. n.* inciting *35/16*.

nothyng *adv.* not at all, in no way *32/32*.

noughty *adj.* evil *8/24*.

o *adj.* one *25/2*.

obeye *v.* ∼ *to* be ruled by *19/15*.

occasyon *n.* pretext, justification (for sinning) *23/14*. ∼ *of* induce- ment to *35/11*.

ocupyeth *pr. 3 sg.* enters into *21/17*.

of *prep.* concerning, about *12/15*, *24/2*; by *19/8*, *36/3*; because of *20/24*; according to, with *20/32*; to *23/26*; in *16/15*, *30/16*; from *39/3*.

offence *n.* stumbling block *29/16*; *pl.* misfortunes *7/6. yn* ∼ *of* trans- gressing against *7/14*.

offyce *n.* use, function *22/28*, *29/7*. *vseth the* ∼ *of* behaves like *3/26*.

offre *v.* expose (oneself) *28/22* (*MED*, *OED* meaning om.).

only *adv.* in *al* ∼ by itself *6/12*.

onswer *v.* explain *8/6*; correspond (to) in number and kind *31/9*.

open *adj.* public *32/13. make* ∼ reveal *9/20*.

operacion *n.* action *11/24*.

opynly *adv.* publicly *10/13*.

oppresse *v.* crush *28/1*.

ordeyned *pp.* conducted *28/16*. ∼ *to* set aside for *39/4*.

ordre *n.* ? civil or public order *18/35* (see note); way of doing things *38/25. maner and* ∼ proper disposition *14/11. ordres and maners* practices, methods of doing things *18/18* (L. 'morum').

ouyr *prep.* in addition to *13/2*.

ouyral *adv.* in every part *14/4*; everywhere *31/5*.

outewarde *adv.* from without *9/36*.

pareyles *n. pl.* furnishings, trap- pings *26/25*.

parsuade *v*. counsel *14/26* (*MED* om.; *OED* 1526).

parteyne *pr. subj.* ～ *to* concern, be used for *22/29*.

partes *n. pl.* members *38/19*, *38/25*.

party *n*. portion (of a book or treatise) *21/2*; *pl*. ways of life, conditions *3/24*.

partyculer *adj*. individual, private *38/27*, *43/10*; *see* **god**.

pass(e) *pr. subj.* passes by *29/13*. ～ *wyth the tyme* make one's way as time passes *29/10* (L. 'tempus pretereant').

peece *v*. quell *38/2*.

peyne *n*. punishment *20/23*; *pl*. *23/27*.

peyseth *pr. 3 sg.* balances *15/9*.

penaunce *n*. punishment *21/9*.

penvrye *n*. lack *18/36*.

perceuer *v*. endure *23/5*; *pr. 3 sg.* *38/24*.

perdureth *pr. 3 sg.* lasts *38/20*.

pertyculer *n*. logic: particular proposition *22/25* (*MED* meaning om.; *OED* 1551). *yn* ～ in individual cases *22/27* (*MED* phr. om.; *OED* 1585).

pestelence *n*. moral wickedness fatal to well-being *9/38*. **pestylence** *20/8*.

pytuously *adv*. compassionately *12/4*; grievously *19/9*.

plukke *v*. ～ *away* snatch, steal *9/32*; *pp*. *18/20*.

plungeth *pr. 3 sg.* throws *30/12*.

poletyke *adj*. prudent *17/26*; public *18/31*.

pollute *ppl. adj.* defiled *21/22*.

portable *adj*. capable *44/11* (*MED, OED* meaning om.; L. 'capaces').

possede *v*. possess *38/13*.

pourveyde *pp*. brought about by planning ahead *8/20*.

practyke *n*. practice, as opposed to theory *14/22*.

precyous *adj*. costly (in lives) *41/11*.

precyously *adv*. expensively *27/29*.

preysed *ppl. adj. as n.* esteemed *24/1*.

preveth *pr. 3 sg.* tests *32/12*; *ppl. adj.* trustworthy *43/25*.

preuyded *pp*. provided *29/2*.

pryce *n*. glory, praise *9/28*.

prykked *ppl. adj.* impelling, inciting *23/25* (*MED, OED* ppl. adj. om.).

princyplees *n. pl.* fundamental assumptions *39/3*. **pryncyples** origins, sources *42/21*.

pryvates *n. pl.* people not holding public office *37/5*.

procede *pr. subj.* error for 'precede' = take precedence over *39/5*.

processe *n*. carrying out *28/18*. *vnto lenger* ～ *of yerys* for the future *8/22*.

proferred *pp*. ～ *to* placed in authority over *24/10* (N **preferred**; L. 'preficiendum').

profytable *adj*. helpful (to) *22/10*; worthy *23/2*.

prolonged *pp*. delayed *35/6*.

promytte *pr. pl.* cause to expect *8/24*.

provicion *n*. foresight *23/28*, *38/8*.

provyde *v*. foresee, make provisions for *38/5* (N adds **for**).

pvnyssyon *n*. punishment *32/9*.

put *pr. pl.* ? keep, ? value *21/26* (see note); *see* **mouthe**.

putrefye *v*. become corrupt morally *32/18* (*MED* meaning om.; *OED* 1526).

qualyte *n*. nature *30/4*; *pl*. four primary qualities (heat, coldness, wetness, dryness) *38/21*.

quenched *pp*. extinguished *9/25*.

quykketh *pr. 3 sg.* gives life to *20/28*.

rad *pp*. read *5/18*. **redde** *5/21*.

rathyr *adv*. more properly *12/5*.

raveynouse *adj.* extremely rapacious *10/10*.

redemyd *pp.* paid for *42/15*.

redy *adj.* close at hand *15/24*.

reduce *v.* bring back (to the mind) *6/7*; restore (to a state or condition) *43/16*; *pr. pl.* bring by constraint or compulsion *20/23*.

refourme *v.* restore *32/24-5*.

refuse *n.* remainder, survivors *40/36* (equivalent of **relyques**, l. 36).

reyseth *pr. 3 sg.* sets in motion *32/13*.

relyques *n. pl.* remainder, survivors *40/36*.

remna(u)nt remainder *14/29, 17/17*.

renneth *pr. 3 sg.* spreads *31/14*.

renomee *n.* fame, glory *18/18*.

renovel *v.* repeat *8/9*.

repentyd *pa. t.* changed His mind *33/22*.

repreuable *adj.* blamed *9/29*.

reproved *pp.* made ineffective *34/22*.

reteyne *v. refl.* keep himself (from slipping) *3/18*; *pa. t.* prevented from departing *6/25*.

returne *v.* reverse *13/26* (see note).

ryght *n.* in *of verrey* ~ rightfully *38/27*.

sad *adj.* profoundly learned *18/15*.

sadnes *n.* firmness, stability *21/2*.

satyffye *v.* meet the wishes of, content *26/9, 38/31* (*OED* chiefly Sc. for 'satisfy').

savoureth *pr. 3 sg.* ~ *yn* tastes with relish *18/24*.

sawes *n. pl.* discourse *22/23*.

sawles *n. pl.* individuals *38/27*.

scharpe *adj.* harsh, merciless *23/25, 42/23*.

schewe *v.* call down (on us) *44/4*; present *13/14*; reveal *14/28, 21/24*; *refl.* reveal oneself *11/11, 23/20, 24/21*; *pr. pl. intr.* are seen *13/19*; *pa. t.* made evident *7/13*; declared *14/23*; appeared *7/15*. *schewest as though pr. 2 sg.* have an appearance that suggests that *7/26*.

schewenge *ppl. adj.* evident *23/21*.

schul(le) *pr. pl.* shall *21/31, 32/8*.

scorneful *adj.* contemptible *21/21* (*OED* 1570).

sece *v.* stop *34/31*.

see *pr. pl.* ~ *before* perceive ahead of time *13/12*.

sees *n. pl.* thrones, dwelling places *16/29*.

seyth(e) *pr. 3 sg.* in *as ho* ~ as they say *1/26, 20/7, 29/9*.

self *refl. pron.* itself *36/19*.

self *adj.* same *10/35*.

semes *pr. impers.* in *me* ~ it seems to me *13/24*. *semeth vs 44/10*.

sence *n.* perception *34/23*.

sentence *n.* opinion *11/20*; judgement *44/2*.

serche *v.* make oneself thoroughly acquainted with *24/27*; seek diligently for *40/10*.

setteth *pr. 3 sg.* ~ *yn mesure* keep in proper balance or proportion *24/6*. **set** *pa. t.* ~ *ap(p)art(e)* dismissed from consideration *7/18, 33/26*; *pp. 13/10*; ~ *at nought* not valued at all *9/29*. *ben* ~ *yn* have gotten power *2/29*.

seurte *n.* means of safety, safeguard *12/16, 14/21*; security *21/2*.

shadowed *pa. t.* obscured *40/28*.

syde *n.* in *in euery* ~ everywhere, i.e., by many *28/4* (L. 'multi').

sygnes *n. pl.* statues, proofs *10/4*.

syngler *adj.* individual, private *38/24*.

syngularly *adv.* particularly *23/16*.

synguler *adj.* private *9/30, 26/19*.

synneth *pr. 3 sg.* ~ *to* sins against *21/33*. *synne to pr. pl. 21/35*.

sytteth *pr. 3 sg. impers.* is not proper *33/5*. **syttynge** *pr. p.* proper *1/5-6*.

slyper *adj.* readily slipping from one's grasp *3/18*.

softly *adv.* in a leisurely manner *32/10*.

softnes *n.* voluptuous living *9/22*.

somtyme *adv.* once *9/20, 17/24*.

sorow *v.* mourn *4/30*.

sownde *pr. pl.* ~ *to* have a connection with *22/14*.

space *n.* time *12/7, 40/26*.

specyalte *n.* particularity or detail in discussion *19/20*.

spectacles *n. pl.* stages or platforms for public exhibitions like hangings *30/14*.

spede *v.* make clear to, assure *39/26* (*OED* meaning om.; L. 'scio expedire').

sperpulyd *pp.* scattered *40/34*.

spiracle *n.* spirit *36/2*.

spyrytes *n. pl.* vital energy *8/17*.

sprongen *ppl. adj.* ~ *owt of* originating from *16/29*.

stablyscheth *pr. 3 sg.* makes stable *16/29*.

stande *pr. pl.* are *20/7*.

states *n. pl.* nobles, princes *1/10*.

sterynge *vbl. n.* provocation *23/13*; *pl. 23/25*.

styrre *v.* incite *38/2*.

straunge *adj.* in ~ *to* far removed from *25/18*.

straungers *n. pl.* foreigners *7/28*.

streynest *pr. 2 sg.* ~ *of* contend against *31/18* (L. 'contendas'; see note).

streyte *adj.* strict *23/25*; stingy *26/11*. **strayte** narrow, i.e., difficult and painful *38/4*.

streytely *adv.* rigorously *25/12*.

strengthe *n.* capacity for moral effort or endurance *22/21*.

study *n.* deliberate effort *9/11*; *pl.* efforts *12/25*.

studyen *pr. pl.* endeavour *38/12*. **study** *pr. subj.* *24/31*.

studyous *adj.* giving careful atten-

tion *42/21* (const. 'for'—*OED* rare, 1553).

studyously *adv.* eagerly *36/22* (*OED* exact meaning om.; L. 'studiosius').

subtele *adj.* involving careful discrimination *37/22*.

subtylte *n.* treachery *9/14*; cunning, craftiness *30/8*.

superfluouse *adj.* immoderate *15/3*.

sustynaunce *n.* support *27/32*.

swelled *pa. t.* became arrogant *6/15*.

swolow *n.* sink (of evil) *19/29*.

tables *n. pl.* ? memorial tablets fixed in a wall; ? written records (*OED* meaning om.) *10/4* (L. 'tabulas').

take *pr. 1 sg.* understand *37/21*. ~ *vppon hym* (*hymself*) make bold to seize or take *21/7, 27/12*.

taught *ppl. adj.* learned *7/27, 30/29*.

temperaunce *n.* mingling in due proportion *38/20*.

tempre *v. refl.* be moderate *5/15*; *pr. 3 sg.* controls *15/5*.

that *rel. pron.* that which *28/2, 35/9, 38/1*.

then *conj.* except *38/2*.

thynges *n. pl.* circumstances *18/19*; reports of those deeds which are to be done *42/7* (L. 'rumores').

thyr *pron. poss.* their *21/23, 28/16, 30/16, 32/14*.

thyr *dem. adv.* there *1/11, 2/2, 2/12, 3/3, 3/25*, etc. (*OED* sp. om.).

thyrto *adv.* to there *21/18*; to it *28/5*.

thys *adj. pl.* these *10/20, 29/10*.

tho *adj.* those *21/16*.

tyme *n.* in *by longe* ~ for a long time *32/12*. *on a* ~ once *4/21*.

to *prep.* with regard to *8/5, 13/3, 24/24, 26/10*; about *19/29*; from *22/24*; for *36/27, 38/14*; so as to bring about *38/25*.

toward *prep.* verging upon *14/2*.

towche *v.* attain *39/18*. **tuched** *pa. t.* concerned *18/13*.

translateth *pr. 3 sg.* transfers *18/4*; *pp.* *18/7*.

trobelous *adj.* vexatious, troublesome *28/23*.

trowe *pr. 1 sg.* hope *34/34*. **trouest** *pr. 2 sg.* believe *20/19*.

trust *n.* hope *28/4*.

trust *v.* ~ to rely on *8/23*, *27/20*.

turne *v.* direct *12/25*; change *34/25*; turn back *34/30*. *is turned to* has become *13/4*.

vncomodyouse *adj.* unprofitable, unpleasant *3/22*.

vndyr *prep.* according to *35/2*.

vndyrstondyng *vbl. n.* ability to understand *18/30*. **vnderstandyng** meaning *35/27*.

vnequyte *n.* unreasonableness, injustice *2/10*, *20/28*.

vnferme *adj.* weak *37/13* (*OED* 1616).

vnhappy *adj.* disastrous, evil *10/20*.

vnholsom *adj.* morally corrupt *13/3*.

vnhonest *adj.* dishonourable *30/17*.

vnyuersal *adj.* in *a man* ~ a man interested in the welfare of all men *24/21* (*OED* no use exactly like this).

vnkynde *adj.* lacking in willingness to acknowledge benefits *44/12*.

vnkyndely *adv.* ungratefully *33/26*.

vnknawen *ppl. adj.* unfamiliar *35/7*.

vnknowyng *adj.* ignorant *32/27*.

vnmesured *ppl. adj.* boundless, vast *29/27*, *31/19*.

vnmevable *adj.* steadfast *29/27*.

vnnethe *adv.* scarcely *12/26*, *40/32*.

vnordenat *adj.* inordinate *15/13*.

vnpyty *n.* wickedness *16/25*.

vnproporcyoned *adj.* not formed in proper proportions *14/4* (*OED* c. 1586).

vnschamefastnes *n.* indecency, scandalousness *21/12*.

vnsyttynge *ppl. adj.* improper *14/15*.

vntaught *adj.* ignorant *7/27*.

vnwysedom *n.* instance of ignorance *8/5*.

vppon *prep.* over *22/30*, *24/15*, *34/29*; with respect to *26/24*.

vse *n.* ? scribal error for 'vice' *37/16* (L. 'peccatum').

vse *v.* take advantage of *28/6*; *pr. 3 sg.* practises *3/26*; *pp.* engaged in *16/23*; *ppl. adj.* usual *30/17*.

vanyssched *pp.* ~ *ynto* disappeared and became worthless *14/21*.

vengable *adj.* cruel, dreadful *10/8*.

very *adj.* mere *19/29*.

vysytacion *n.* coming to exert power (of God) *33/1*.

voyde *adj.* vain *42/15*.

wayted *pa. t.* ~ *aftyr* waited for *19/19*.

walled places *n. pl. phr.* fortified cities *41/8*.

wey *n.* in *whyche* ~ wherever *43/8*. *by* ~ *of* by means of *21/18*; see **loke**.

weymentynges *n. pl.* laments *7/24*.

wenyng *ppl. adj.* believing *27/24*.

wepable *adj.* lamentable *40/34*.

whatsomeuyr *pron.* no matter what *10/22*.

whereas *rel. adv. conj.* where, when *7/13*, *27/27*.

wherto *adv.* for what purpose *32/30*.

whyche *pron.* those who (lacks antecedent) *26/17*.

wynnyng *vbl. n.* getting of wealth *19/28*.

wyth *prep.* by *8/31*, *9/3*; without loss of *28/21*.

wythdrewe *pa. t.* took away *18/1*. **wythdrough** caused to decrease *26/24-5*.

wodenes *n.* madness *19/4*.

wolde *pr. subj.* desire *37/13*; ordain *44/3*.

wonderfull *adj.* disastrous, evil *23/8* (*OED* meaning only under 'wonder'; see note).

woode *adj.* mad with fury *7/16*.

wrakke *n.* shipwreck *14/3*. go to ∼ be shipwrecked *13/17*.

wreth *n.* anger *4/22*.

wurschipful *adj.* bringing distinction *9/26*.

yef(f) *conj.* if *35/19*, *38/25*. **yif** *43/6*.

yeue *pr. subj.* devote or surrender (oneself) *16/10*; *pp.* produced *25/28*; *see* **delygence**.

ȝele *n.* fervent devotion *4/21*.

LIST OF NAMES

Anaxagaras Anaxagoras *21/4* (see note).

Camilus Furius Camillus *11/20*.

Cartage *40/19*.

Caton *11/26*.

Charlemayn *34/7–8*.

Clodryk ? Childeric, King of the Franks *34/7* (L. 'Clodoveus').

Clotayre King of the Franks *34/7*.

Dagobet Dagobert, King of the Franks *34/7*.

Fabyus Fabius Maximus *26/28*.

Grece *19/5*.

Grekes *18/1*, *40/33*.

Hamo Hanno the Great *40/15* (L. 'Hannonis').

Hanybal *6/15*, *40/16*.

Iues Jews *33/18*.

Lybye Libya *11/29*.

Lucyna the goddess of childbirth *8/21*.

Manlyus Torquatus *43/20* (**Mawlyus** SJ; cf. **Mavlius**, *The Quadrilogue Invective*, *226/30*).

Marcus Curcyus M. Curtius *12/1*.

Perse Persia *40/26*.

Phylostrate Philostratus *19/4*.

Pypyn Pepin, King of the Franks *34/7*.

Roome *6/16*, *12/2*, *19/6*.

Ro(o)meyns *18/1*, *40/24*.

Salust *16/10*.

Scypyo Affrycan Scipio Africanus Major *6/14–15*.

Socrates *4/12*.

Tyrence Terence *14/15*.

Tytus Lyvyus Livy *6/29*.

Troye *40/32*.

Tullyus Cicero *19/6*.

Vtyke Utica *11/29*.

Valery Valerius Publicola *26/22* (see note).

Varo Marcus Terentius Varro *3/2* (see note).

Ӡerces Xerxes *14/22*. **Ӡerses** *40/26*.